An Enchantment
OF BIRDS

RICHARD CANNINGS

Illustrations by Donald Gunn

An Enchantment
OF BIRDS

MEMORIES FROM A BIRDER'S LIFE

David
Suzuki
Foundation

GREYSTONE BOOKS

Douglas & McIntyre Publishing Group
Vancouver/Toronto/Berkeley

Copyright © 2007 by Richard Cannings

07 08 09 10 11 5 4 3 2 1

Greystone Books
A division of Douglas & McIntyre Ltd.
2323 Quebec Street, Suite 201
Vancouver, British Columbia
Canada V5T 4S7
www.greystonebooks.com

David Suzuki Foundation
219–2211 West 4th Avenue
Vancouver, British Columbia
Canada V6K 4S2

Library and Archives Canada Cataloguing in Publication
Cannings, Richard J. (Richard James)
An enchantment of birds : memoirs from a birder's life / Richard
Cannings ; illustrations by Donald Gunn.

ISBN: 978-1-55365-235-9

1. Cannings, Richard J. (Richard James). 2. Birds—North America.
3. Bird watching—North America. 4. Birds—Anecdotes.
5. Bird watchers—Canada—Biography. I. Gunn, Donald, 1960– II. Title
QL677.5.C365 2007   598.072'347   C2006-907002-4

Copy editing by Iva Cheung
Jacket design by Jessica Sullivan
Interior design by Lisa Hemingway
Jacket image © csaimages.com
Illustrations by Donald Gunn

Printed and bound in Canada by Friesens
Printed on paper that does not contain materials from trees of old-growth forests
Distributed in the U.S. by Publishers Group West

We gratefully acknowledge the financial support of the Canada Council for the Arts,
the British Columbia Arts Council, and the Government of Canada through the Book
Publishing Industry Development Program (BPIDP) for our publishing activities.

TABLE OF CONTENTS

PREFACE

$\mathcal{I}$ HAVE ALWAYS BEEN enchanted with birds. There was no moment of epiphany—the sighting of a brightly colored tanager that piqued my curiosity about its identity or a close encounter with an eagle that let me see the world through avian eyes. Many of my birding colleagues can point to such an event, a day that divides their life into before birds and after birds. But birds were always part of my life. The origin of this fascination is perhaps obvious—I was born into a family that lived and breathed nature. We talked about birds over dinner, my parents searched out rare flowers on family outings, and my father wrote down everything in his diary of nature notes.

I've often wondered what got my father interested in birds, since his mother was not an outdoors person at all and he never knew his own father. My grandfather had immigrated to Canada from the slums of Bristol and succumbed to the double scourge of pneumonia and tuberculosis when my father was only two. My grandfather kept a diary as well and wrote of Sunday walks with his brothers and friends through the English countryside.

Although they often had barely enough money to buy food, he and his brothers managed to save enough between them to buy a guide to British wildflowers. When he moved to British Columbia, his diary became mostly brief accounts of what work he managed to find in the local mines or ranches and how little he was paid for it, but some of his journal entries mention that he was collecting butterflies to send back to the natural history museum in Bristol.

My father came to serious birding later in life and claims that the interest was sparked by childhood hikes through the wild prairies and woodlands, and he even remembers a series of bird identification cards printed in cigarette packages that caught his eye (though he never smoked). As I grew up I found myself keeping a notebook like my father's, jotting down the birds I saw each day. My two brothers are both professional biologists and keen naturalists, and my son is now a good birder as well. So perhaps there is some genetic link to our attraction to nature, a group of genes that predispose one to curiosity about the world and the creatures we share it with.

Whatever the origins of this interest, it is indeed an enchantment. Once the spell has been cast, you forever experience the world differently, eyeing forests as if you were a woodpecker looking for nesting snags, subconsciously counting migrating geese as they fly overhead, trying to decide if that hooting owl is a male or female. Although some might think that these habits border on an obsession, I feel that the world would be a better place if we all looked more closely at birds and tried to understand how they perceive their surroundings.

I'm often asked what my favorite bird is, and I always have difficulty coming up with a single candidate. The birds in this book are perhaps a short list of my favorites, some because of special experiences I've had with them, some because their songs touch my soul, some because they simply do very interesting things. Since I grew up and still live in western Canada, many of the species chosen have a western flavor, but most are widespread and familiar to birders across North America. I hope their stories will touch you as well and perhaps begin to cast a spell that will last a lifetime.

WESTERN MEADOWLARK

*M*Y EARLIEST MEMORIES are of meadowlarks. Their songs rang through my open bedroom window as the morning sky brightened, and they have become etched in my mind as a coordinate of home. Whereas the hypnotic sounds of crickets and lisping sprinklers were my lullabies as a very young boy, meadowlarks were my alarm clocks, waking me to the warm summer mornings. Their songs are the anthem of the grasslands, as much a part of life in the West as the taste of saskatoon berries, the smell of sagebrush after a thunderstorm, and the color of the evening sky above the black mountains in the summer twilight.

Just before I was born, my parents built a house in a new rural subdivision carved out of wild bunchgrass. Before our family owned the land it was meadowlark country, and for the first five or six years that we lived there the birds came back to the yard each spring, until the young apple orchard turned the prairie into a deciduous woodland and they had to look elsewhere to nest. Western meadowlarks are birds of the grasslands and cannot tolerate forests, though they will happily sing from a ponderosa pine growing high and lonesome amid the grass. But for those few years the meadowlarks were a big part of my backyard, the males singing from the freshly planted apple trees, the young riding on the back of the tractor as it mowed the long grass in midsummer.

My brothers and I spent much of our childhood "across the fence," playing on the unplowed grasslands of the Penticton Indian Reserve. In winter we would toboggan down the steep slopes of the hills, using the snowdrifts behind each sagebrush as jumps. When spring came we looked for the first buttercup, then, when the ground was yellow with them, tried to find the one with the most petals. I learned which plants were tastiest and was particularly fond of the tangy flavor of a distinctive gray, grass-like leaf that came directly out of the spring soil. Only later did I learn to my embarrassment that I had been desecrating one of the most beautiful plants of the grassland, the mariposa lily. We would push toy trucks around the clumps of prickly pear cactus, hide in the rose thickets, and try—always unsuccessfully—to sneak up on coyotes. Occasionally we would see more uncommon birds—a flock of gray partridge exploding from the shrubs, a burrowing owl standing watchfully next to its subterranean nest, or a long-billed curlew calling mournfully in the distance—but we were always surrounded by meadowlarks. Their songs were the soundtrack of our young lives.

Loud and melodic, meadowlark songs sail through the dry air, advertising the presence of a male with a territory. One might think that meadowlarks and other grassland songbirds are at a disadvantage when compared with forest birds in that they don't have any high trees from which to broadcast their songs far and wide. But the wide open spaces are an advantage for being both seen and heard—there are no trees to get in the way. To get a high singing site, many grassland birds—the sky lark is a famous example—simply fly up into the air, giving long songs while they are mere specks against the blue sky. Male meadowlarks have a flight song, but it is not as musical (to the human ear) as the song they give while standing on fence posts or other perches.

Their beautiful songs probably gave meadowlarks their name, but they are not related to other larks. The lark family is more or less confined to the Old World—Eurasia and Africa—with only one representative in North America, the horned lark. Meadowlarks are members of the family Icteridae, a large and diverse group of New World birds that includes the blackbirds and orioles. Again, neither is related to their Old World namesakes.

To add visual impact to their songs, many grassland birds have striking plumage patterns that are visible only from below. Most birds (indeed, most animals) have a characteristic dark-above-light-below color pattern that is clearly advantageous when they want to blend in with either the dark ground when seen from above or the pale sky when seen from below. A meadow-dwelling cousin of the meadowlark, the bobolink, has a display plumage that is the complete opposite of this normal pattern: the males are jet black below and mostly white above, making them easily visible while they chatter out the song for which they are named. Meadowlarks are almost invisible from above; their pale brown plumage speckled with black and white is indistinguishable from the dry grass they hide in. But seen from below they are a sight to behold—eye-popping yellow breasts set off with a bold black V necklace and bright white outer tail feathers that flash against the sky.

Not coincidentally, the meadowlark plumage pattern is roughly repeated in the horned lark, which shares many North American grasslands with meadowlarks. There is a group of birds in African grasslands, the longclaws, which look even more like meadowlarks—the color patterns are essentially identical, and only a more slender body form and longer hind claw set the longclaws apart. The longclaws, members of the pipit family, have orange- and red-breasted species as well—a pattern repeated in several meadowlark species found in South American grasslands. The meadowlarks and longclaws are a textbook example of convergent evolution. They are totally unrelated species that have evolved very similar plumages in response to similar evolutionary forces—in this case the need to be seen and recognized while performing courtship flight songs in wide-open spaces.

Most grassland birds nest directly on the ground for obvious reasons—there are few bushes or trees in sight. A meadowlark nest is tucked deep into a hollow beside a clump of grass, hidden completely by dried grass that bends over the nest and its entrance. The female sits so tightly on the nest that few are ever found; I have seen only two in my life despite many days of searching. The nests I have found were discovered accidentally when I literally stepped on the incubating females, causing them to explode away on those short meadowlark wings. Luckily I didn't damage the nest contents. Because predators such as skunks and coyotes would love to find the nestlings, the adults are very wary of approaching the nest when feeding their young. If you ever try to find a meadowlark nest by watching an adult with a beak full of grasshoppers, you will find yourself in a long waiting game, the bird patiently giving warning calls to its mate, knowing you will soon tire of the game and go away.

A more unfortunate characteristic that almost all grassland species in North America share is declining populations. Once each year I get up very early on a June morning and do a Breeding Bird Survey along a standard 25-mile-long route in the Okanagan Valley. I leave home about 3:45 AM and drive through the dark to the starting point, getting my data sheets ready under cold, clear skies while listening to the first birds of the day—robins, bluebirds, juncos. Up on the hill, a poorwill gives one last series of calls before going to sleep for the day. I have to begin the survey at exactly 4:20 AM, listen for three minutes at the first stop, noting what I see and hear, then drive a half-mile to the next stop, and repeat the procedure. The survey takes more than four hours to complete, and by the fiftieth and final stop I am certainly ready for either a strong coffee or a nap. It takes a lot of motivation to get out of bed and get the survey done each year, but the results are well worth the effort—a long-term data set that tells biologists more about bird population trends than any other program in North America.

When I began this survey in 1973 I used to count about fifty meadowlarks along my route—they were the commonest species on my list. For the past six years I've only heard about twenty each time, and robins have replaced them at the top of the list. Data from almost three hundred similar surveys from across western Canada show the same result—there are only about half the number of western meadowlarks now that there were thirty years ago. Other grassland birds—sharp-tailed and sage grouse, ferruginous hawks, burrowing owls, horned larks, Sprague's pipits, and longspurs—have declined to equal or greater degrees. In fact, as a group, grassland birds are declining faster than the birds associated with any other habitat in North America. What is it about grasslands?

Perhaps the simplest explanation is that grasslands are easy targets for development. There are no trees to cut down, no swamps to drain—just flatten the land out a bit and build the houses, as my parents did fifty years ago. But it is agriculture, not urban development, that is the biggest threat to grasslands. Across most of the West, all farmers have to do is plow the fertile soil, plant their crops, and pray for rain. Over the last century, water diversions have provided ample irrigation for the development of dry grasslands, saving the need for prayer in many areas. The statistics are clear-cut: 99 percent of the moister grasslands of the West, the tallgrass prairies, are gone forever, and about 70 percent of drier grasslands have disappeared as well. The latter are suffering another onslaught—that of invasive weeds that have taken over much of the bunchgrass hills of the West. When I walk across some of the pockets of grass left in southern British Columbia I'm often hard-pressed to see any native plants other than scattered sagebrush and rabbitbrush—the rest is Dalmatian toadflax, diffuse knapweed, sulfur cinquefoil, and cheatgrass.

Meadowlarks are highly migratory in the northern part of their range; in October I often kick up a small flock in the golden grass as they gather for the flight south. The habitat loss that Canadian meadowlarks suffer may be exacerbated while they are wintering in the southwestern United States or northern Mexico. Those reaching Arizona may find condos where grass grew the previous year, and those headed for Texas and Mexico are often confronted with intensively cultivated crops such as cotton. While the ground is frozen in winter the Canadian grasslands are almost completely empty of birdlife. But as the spring sun melts the snow and the buttercups bloom, western meadowlarks are among the first birds to reclaim the awakening land. With the warmth in the air, the flashes of yellow, and the clear notes of meadowlark song, hope returns to the West.

WESTERN KINGBIRD

*M*Y BROTHERS AND I were avid birders from a young age, and it was probably inevitable that we would become biologists when we grew up. But the summer of 1969 clinched that career path for me. That year my twin brother, Syd, and I became hooked on a program run by the Provincial Museum in Victoria—the British Columbia Nest Records Scheme. The idea was simple enough: participants filled out a file card for every nest that they found, describing the nest and noting the dates it was active as well as the number of eggs or young at each visit. It was a popular program back then and remains so today, having built up the largest regional database on breeding birds in North America.

Nest records schemes provide invaluable information for conservation biologists. If the population of a species is declining, the first question these biologists ask themselves is "What's happening on the breeding grounds?" Nest cards can provide clues to the answer—fewer eggs being laid, fewer young fledged, or fewer nests found. They also tell us where birds nest—in particular trees that might be affected by forestry or development projects, or in a certain type of meadow that is vulnerable to agricultural activities.

Syd and I had helped our parents keep track of nests in 1967 and 1968, but in 1969 we decided to take on the project by ourselves and really find a lot of nests. We set up a friendly competition with our schoolmate Doug Leighton (now a renowned nature photographer) to see who could fill out the most nest cards. While school was in session we spent every weekend looking for nests, cajoling our parents to drive us to a different spot each day. The instructions sent out with the nest cards urged participants to visit nests several times to see if they were successful, but in our youthful enthusiasm we were simply after numbers of nests, though we rechecked nests when we could. After school was out we spent every day on our quest, hiking into the grasslands across the fence, where we found out how difficult it was to find meadowlark nests, or up into the hills west of Penticton. I learned all the Latin names of the local birds that year—you had to fill that in on every card— and more about the breeding biology of birds than a university course could have ever taught me. By the end of that summer Syd and I had carded 837 nests (Doug found 1,002, but that's another story) and biology had become my life.

Our favorite birds that year were western kingbirds. These large flycatchers share the dry grasslands and open ponderosa pine forests of western valleys and plains with the meadowlarks. Like the meadowlarks, they are bright yellow below and have prominent white outer tail feathers, but there the similarity ends. Being flycatchers, kingbirds don't have a complex song like most songbirds; indeed, the songs and calls they give

are completely innate, coded by genetic material. Other songbirds have to learn the song of their species from their fathers or
neighbors. Kingbirds have a simple bickering chatter that is as
much a backdrop to summer mornings in the West as meadowlark song, though admittedly not as aesthetically pleasing.
Kingbirds also differ from the shy meadowlarks in that they are
highly pugnacious, diving and snapping at any possible predator that dares venture near their nest. This behavior has given
them their English name, as well as their Latin name: *Tyrannus*.

But the real reason Syd and I liked western kingbirds
so much in the summer of 1969 was that their nests were
dead easy to find. Before technology came to the West, kingbirds nested on large branches of big trees—ponderosa pines
and cottonwoods—that dotted the dry grasslands, but once
the telegraph arrived many switched to the power poles that
lined the roads and railways. Racking up a big number of
nests was as easy as getting Dad to drive along a road while
Syd and I kept track of each nest, quickly noting whether it
was behind the transformer of a power pole or nestled on the
insulators, and whether the adult was still incubating the eggs
or feeding nestlings. We didn't get much data on the number
of eggs or young in each nest—they were too high to look
into safely—but did find out how far north the birds nested
in British Columbia (Alexandria, between Williams Lake and
Quesnel) and what the peak time of nesting was (the date
June 9 sticks in my mind as being when most kingbirds were
sitting on eggs).

On one of our hikes into the Okanagan hills, Syd and I
found a western kingbird nest on a pole carrying television

cable lines to the top of the mountain behind our home. Although the nest looked freshly built, we were surprised that no adults materialized to attack us as all kingbirds would. When we got to the base of the pole we saw the reason— two small young kingbirds, wearing only pinfeathers, lay on the ground, covered in ants. The adults were gone, probably giving up the nest for lost when they found it empty after an attack by a nest robber such as a raven or magpie. Usually the female broods the young faithfully while the male perches nearby to chase off any intruders. Because kingbird nests are so exposed to view, eggs and nestlings are often lost to predators despite the vigorous defense mounted by the adults. Whatever the circumstances in this case, the young birds weren't going to survive another day unless we took them in.

So we carried them home in our pockets and named them Chuck and Dave after a line in a Beatles song popular at the time. (Now, I should say here, "Don't try this at home"; raising nestling birds by hand is extremely difficult and also illegal without a permit. If you do find a lonely-looking young bird, call your local wildlife rescue association.) Dave unfortunately died within a day, but Chuck grew up to be good natural kingbird. While he was still growing feathers, we fed him a mixture of mashed bugs, boiled egg, and ground beef, pushed down his throat with a toothpick.

We worried at first about how to teach Chuck to fly and feed in the manner of kingbirds, but we needn't have been concerned. Like their simple songs, most of what kingbirds (and other birds) do is innate. All members of the flycatcher family, kingbirds included, sally out from a perch and catch passing insects with a loud snap of their flat bills. Chuck picked up this behavior automatically and would sit on the telephone line into our house while we flicked beetle-sized chunks of ground beef upward. From the day he could fly, he never missed a flying meal, snatching the tidbits as if he'd been doing it for years. After a few days the fledglings from a kingbird nest down our driveway joined him in the feeding ritual. And sometime in early August they all disappeared, presumably off to their wintering grounds along the Pacific coast of Central America. Western kingbirds are early migrants, leaving at the height of summer as soon as the young birds can fly strongly.

I sometimes muse about Chuck's fate, wondering whether he ever returned to the Okanagan Valley. I must admit I've never encountered a kingbird since that showed any affection toward me; any that I approach either timidly fly away or dive angrily and noisily at me as they would at any potential predator. So perhaps Chuck never made it to the tropics and back, or perhaps he really did become a proper kingbird, a tyrant of the hot summer grasslands.

EVENING GROSBEAK

*T*HE OTHER BIRD we cared for as boys was George, a male evening grosbeak. George had flown into our living room window one winter day and suffered a severe concussion. Evening grosbeaks are large, striking finches with surprisingly large bills—hence the name. The males have a yellow-olive body with a black head and a bright yellow headband, whereas the females are more brownish-gray. The colorful plumage and large bills can lead some people to jump to conclusions—I've had calls from excited neighbors telling me that they have a flock of parrots in their backyard.

Evening grosbeaks get their name from the early—and mistaken—belief that they sing only in the evening. In a family famous for its songsters (including the canary), evening grosbeaks are unusual in that they do not have a real song at all but apparently give repeated loud call notes to advertise themselves and their territory. For such a common, colorful, and noisy bird, surprisingly little is known about their breeding biology. In all my years of nest-searching I have never found a nest but often see pairs at my bird feeders with newly fledged young.

When we first found George, he was unconscious on the front deck. His head hung limply—a sign that many people would interpret as a broken neck. In fact, a bird has such a supple neck with many vertebrae (thirteen or more, compared to seven in mammals) that it is very difficult to break it in an accident. But once its neck muscles stop working, a bird's head hangs very limply, mimicking a broken neck. The thin skull of birds does not offer much protection in a collision, so most serious impacts result in concussion if not death. We checked for vital signs—his heart was still beating—and placed him in a warm, dark place: a tissue-filled shoebox. Within an hour he was awake but still groggy. We nursed him back to health over the next few weeks, feeding him Russian olive berries and sunflower seeds.

In those days, I associated evening grosbeaks with winter—small flocks would arrive in the late fall and take up residence in the groves of Russian olives along the shores of Okanagan Lake. The Russian olive, introduced from Eurasia, is not an olive at all. It is a close relative of the native wolf-willow and shares with that species the long, silvery-gray leaves and small, aromatic yellow flowers. Unlike the shrub-like wolf-willow, the Russian olive grows to tree size. It produces white berries in fall that are unpalatable for humans, being dry and mealy with a large single seed. But the berries are favorites of many birds in winter, especially robins, waxwings, and bluebirds. Those birds eat the mealy pulp; only grosbeaks can make use of the big pit.

It was remarkable to watch George eat—his large bill handled the berries and seeds with great dexterity. When eating a Russian olive berry, he would quickly extract the large pit by rolling the berry with his tongue while shearing the pulp off with the sharp edge of his mandible. He would then settle the seed into the grooves of his palate and crunch it with a powerful bite. Sunflower seeds were handled by getting them into a sideways position along the edge of his bill, then deftly cracking them open, the shells falling to the floor and the meat going down his throat.

When I returned to live in the Okanagan Valley in 1995 after a twenty-five-year absence, I was surprised to find that evening grosbeaks were more difficult to find in winter but instead were a common summer bird in local backyards. The flocks arrived in spring, consuming great quantities of sunflower seeds from the feeders, disappeared for the month of June (presumably going into the forests to nest), then reappeared in late summer and fall with their young. My wife had a nature store in Penticton that sold wild birdseed; because of the voracious flocks of grosbeaks she sold more birdseed in summer than she did in winter.

Then, around the year 2000, things changed completely. Evening grosbeaks became even rarer in winter, and the summer flocks vanished as well. This phenomenon wasn't just local; year after year the numbers reported on Christmas Bird Counts and Breeding Bird Surveys dwindled across the continent. By 2005 numbers of evening grosbeaks were so low that concern was being voiced about the species by biologists and birders alike. Finches in general are notorious for moving around the continent, looking for good food supplies, but there didn't seem to be high numbers of evening grosbeaks anywhere. Where had they gone? Were they simply nesting quietly in the northern forests away from the prying eyes of birders and biologists? Were seed crops in the forest poor? The answer may well lie not with berries, but with bugs.

For a species so clearly specialized in eating large seeds, it may be surprising to learn that one of the favorite summer foods of evening grosbeaks is a caterpillar—the larva of the spruce budworm moth. Spruce budworms are one of the most important pests of boreal forests across North America. There are several species, but they can all produce serious infestations—often lasting more than a decade—that can affect millions of hectares of fir and spruce and dramatically affect bird populations. Many bird species—especially warblers—key in on the caterpillars and their populations rise quickly. One of these infestations lasted from 1966 to 1992 in eastern Canada, and another occurred from 1978 to the late 1990s in British Columbia.

Before 1960 evening grosbeaks were very irregular visitors to eastern North America; in fact, their official name in Quebec is *le grosbec errant*—the wandering grosbeak. As soon as the spruce budworm populations began to climb, evening grosbeaks moved into eastern Canada on a more permanent basis and began to build their numbers as well. For more than twenty years, birders in Quebec and the Maritimes once excited to see a few individual grosbeaks were seeing thousands on their counts. The grosbeak populations peaked in 1992, then crashed as the caterpillars disappeared. A similar pattern occurred in British Columbia. I remember driving through the western side of Manning Park in the north

Cascades in 1979 and seeing two spectacular sights: the huge areas of gray, caterpillar-killed Douglas-firs and the clouds of grosbeaks flying off the Hope-Princeton highway where they had come to gather grit and salt.

It seems then that the low numbers of evening grosbeaks across the continent may have resulted from coincident lows in outbreaks of the different populations of budworm. Although the drop in budworm infestations was good news for forest-ers, it was bad news for grosbeaks. Forest managers spend a great deal of time and money battling budworms, but at least one scientific paper—called "How much is an evening gros-beak worth?"—raised the idea that perhaps natural controls can be cost-effective. However, when climatic and forest con-ditions are right, there is little any bird population can do to stop the budworm population from exploding. But wide-scale spray programs only seem to dampen the outbreaks and may even prolong them, whereas a single evening grosbeak, gob-bling over a thousand caterpillars every day, can protect a lot of foliage from destruction.

BOHEMIAN WAXWING

*N*OVEMBER IS A very gray month in my Okanagan Valley childhood memory. We had finished picking all the apples, and the Halloween frosts and autumn winds had stripped the leaves from the trees. Days were often raw and cold; rain squalls sliding down the mountain valleys turned into the first snow flurries of winter. I think of November 11 as the usual day of the first snowfall, but that is probably because we had to stand outside for the Remembrance Day service at the Penticton cenotaph on that day every year, and the few times it did snow during the service were etched into my frostbitten mind.

Most of the southbound migrants had left by late October—the big flocks of robins had passed through, and only a few Audubon's warblers and ruby-crowned kinglets were still chipping in the garden trees. The backyard bird diversity was decidedly reduced—only quail, woodpeckers, chickadees, finches, and a few others remained. Then the northern birds came. As the snow turned the lawn white and I hurriedly raked the last of the yellow leaves, there was a sudden rush of wings and another gray cloud surrounded me, this one a living cloud of birds. Hundreds swirled to a landing on the big mountain-ash tree, then lifted off suddenly for another nervous go-round. Finally they settled on the mountain-ash, their high trilling calls filling the cold air as they devoured the bright orange berries. After filling themselves, they retired to the tops of our neighbor's big Lombardy poplars. The birds were so thick on the white branches it looked like the trees had miraculously leafed out again.

These were bohemian waxwings, elegant birds of the northern forests. A quick look showed that they were not the drab gray birds I noted as they flew quickly by. Their smooth, silky plumage offset with white and yellow racing stripes on the wings and a jaunty crest make them one of the handsomest of birds. Waxwings are named for the striking red spots at the ends of some of their wing feathers, which look for all the world like droplets of sealing wax. Only adults have these red spots and males have more than females, so they are likely a strong signal of a worthy mate. The species gets the "bohemian" moniker from its gypsy-like habit of wandering in winter, when large flocks roam the continent looking for good crops of fruits and berries. A smaller species, the cedar waxwing, moves north into southern Canada in summer, then retreats into the United States for the winter. Both species have a smooth plumage and jaunty crest.

In 1995 I rafted down the Firth River in the northern Yukon, a memorable trip that took me from the taiga woodlands of the British Mountains to the pack ice of the Beaufort Sea. We saw caribou, grizzly bears, wolves, musk oxen, and a million mosquitoes, and of course we saw birds. This was in June, when the Arctic is filled with birds frantically feasting on the insect bounty of the North. Although the summer is short north of the Arctic Circle, the days go on forever, and the birds are there to take advantage of this. They can feed their young around the clock if they like, but usually take a break in the early morning hours—about midnight to three o'clock—to rest before the summer festival continues.

A few of these birds—such as the ravens and ptarmigan—stay all year round in the Arctic, but most migrate south to more moderate climes for the winter. Whereas the sandpipers, plovers, and terns fly all the way to South America, and the warblers migrate to Central America, some—like the bohemian waxwings—are "short-distance" migrants and find southern Canada warm enough. We saw small flocks of these birds all along the forested sections of the river, individuals flying out over the water to snatch emerging stoneflies and caddisflies from the air. These birds were just beginning to nest, for waxwings are late nesters compared with most other songbirds. Whereas other species time their egg-laying so that the young are being fed when insect abundance begins to peak in June; waxwings wait a few weeks so that they can feed their young summer berries that ripen in July.

Many species of birds eat berries—robins and starlings are well known for their love of cherries and grapes in the orchards and vineyards around my home in the Okanagan Valley. But waxwings are real berry specialists and are even choosy about the fruits they eat. Berries are designed to attract

birds, trading the cost of a good meal for the service of trans-
porting the seeds. Many berries are plump and sugary—most
commercial fruits have been developed from that group—
whereas others provide birds with a fatty (for example, sumac
and olives) or even waxy (for example, myrtles) meal. Robins
and starlings will eat whatever berry or fruit is easily available,
but waxwings, when they have a choice, always choose berries
with a high sugar content.

Their favorite food in my neighborhood is the orange
berry of the mountain-ash, also known as the rowan tree. In
the mountain forests above my home, waxwings are highly
attracted to juniper berries. Whatever source of berries they
find, they often stay just long enough to harvest it all, and
when there are five hundred birds in the flock it doesn't take
long to pick an entire treeful of berries. Fortunately for waxwings, food is never in short supply in my neighborhood—
if the mountain-ash runs out, there are always the orchard
blocks with unpicked golden delicious or vineyards full of
grapes left for the icewine harvest. If the berry crop is totally
gone by spring, waxwings can tide themselves over to summer with other sources of sugar, including the sweet sap drip-
ping from maple and birch trunks, protein-rich buds, and
blossoms. Flocks will also attack infestations of scale insects,
thoroughly cleaning trees of this problem.

The berries pass through their bodies very quickly—
waxwings have relatively short intestines—and the seeds
and undigested pulp are defecated in brightly colored droppings. I remember one night I stayed at a friend's house in
Nelson, B.C., and parked beneath a large poplar at the end

of the driveway, not realizing that it was the favorite roosting tree for the local waxwing flock. When I awoke in the morning my car was covered in a thick orange coat of congealed mountain-ash berries. I had to go through the car wash twice just to see out the windshield properly.

Sugary berries are an excellent source of energy in winter and well-fed waxwings quickly put on a healthy layer of fat. But the tasty berries have a couple of challenges associated with them. Their high sugar concentrations—particularly in dried berries late in winter—require the birds to drink more water to maintain proper fluid balance in their bodies. This feat can be tricky in midwinter when all the normal sources of water are often frozen, so waxwings are noted for regularly eating snow. The second problem increases as winter progresses as well—the sugars in the fruit often begin to ferment, producing significant amounts of alcohol. I remember looking out the kitchen window once to see a small flock of waxwings lolling about on the lawn, clearly inebriated. We brought the drunk birds inside to protect them from the neighborhood cats while they sobered up. Interestingly, waxwings have evolved with this alcohol problem and have developed metabolic pathways to deal with alcohol much more quickly than other birds. They can break down ethanol more than three times as fast as starlings can. Waxwings also have unusually large livers, perhaps an adaptation related to this process.

Bohemian waxwing populations seem to be stable or increasing across North America. They are almost impossible to count on their breeding grounds in the vast boreal forests in the northwestern part of the continent, but the numbers of them moving south each winter shows an unsteady increase. Each population peak is followed by a year or more of low numbers, then another peak, usually higher than the last. This slow increase starting in the 1970s is mirrored by the population trend of the cedar waxwing. Since cedar waxwings are well counted in summer, we can guess that the population increase in bohemian waxwings is real as well; biologists speculate that it is directly related to the banning of DDT in 1972.

Bohemian waxwings are usually the most abundant birds tallied on my local Christmas Bird Count in Penticton, with more than two thousand seen on average. Then in the year 2000, for the first time in over forty years of counts, none were seen at all. Waxwings eventually did show up in the area in January, about two months late. Perhaps it was a result of global warming, perhaps just a good year for berries in northern Canada. This is one species we will be watching for clues indicating broadscale changes in the North.

CALIFORNIA QUAIL

*I*N THE OKANAGAN Valley there is a bird so common and distinctive that it has become a regional symbol, appearing on city coats-of-arms, wine labels, and postcards: the California quail. It is such an integral part of the valley scene that most people would be surprised to learn that it is a recent immigrant, introduced to the valley in the early 1900s from its native range of California and Oregon.

Quail flourished in the newly planted orchards and surrounding sagebrush, and by the time I was born they had become a permanent fixture of the new ecosystem. In winter large coveys scuttled from bush to bush across our lawn, attracted by the wheat my father scattered for them every morning. I heard their assembly call daily, a loud, clear *cuh-*CAH*-cow!* (or *Cho-*PA*-ka!* as my son says, using the name of a popular local birding site). In spring the unmated males perched on prominent posts and proclaimed *Coow!* to the world, hoping to attract a female.

California quail belong to that large group of birds that includes grouse, pheasants, turkeys, and chickens. Some general characteristics of the group are that males tend to be more colorful than females, put on elaborate courtship displays, and engage in a rather polygamous lifestyle. As a rule, males don't have anything to do with family life, leaving the nesting and brood-rearing duties entirely to the female. Since the young are precocial and can feed themselves shortly after hatching, this arrangement isn't too much of a problem for the females.

However, the quail of North and South America break most of those rules and are separated into their own family. Although male California quail are somewhat more colorful than females, both sexes have a jaunty topknot that gives them a comic air as they forage on my lawn. Males form long-lasting, monogamous pair-bonds with their mates and take a very active role in raising their families. They don't usually incubate the eggs but are always standing close by to raise the alarm if a potential predator wanders into the neighborhood. And if the female is killed during the nesting period, the male will take over incubation duties so that the brood will survive.

In 1968 my older brother, Rob, got a summer job with a graduate student who was studying quail around Summerland, just north of our home. Whenever I could I would go out in the field with them, excited by the prospect that someone could actually make a living by watching birds and finding nests. The student, Daryl Sherman, caught the quail in an ingeniously simple trap—a low, chicken-wire cage erected over some scattered grain. The quail had to push up on the door to get in, then couldn't lift it up (or even find it) when they had had their fill. Daryl and Rob banded the birds with

unique combinations of color bands so that they could track the movements of coveys throughout the area. Daryl had a Brittany spaniel named Sniff who was trained to point quail but chased other birds such as pheasant and chukar that he came across. When Sniff found some quail we would read off the band combinations—for example, red over blue on right, green over silver on left—then look in a field book to see which covey we were watching.

The following winter was the harshest one of the half-century. I distinctly remember the Christmas Bird Count that year. In those days the Penticton count was always held on Boxing Day, December 26. The day started off with temperatures just below freezing and light snow falling, but the mercury dropped through the day, and by the time we had counted up our daily totals it was -10°c and close to a foot of snow was on the ground. The Arctic air kept filling the valley from the north, and by the afternoon of December 30 an all-time record low of -27.2°c had been set in Penticton.

The quail began to suffer immediately. They had to feed frantically to maintain their body temperature in the Arctic air, but the snow had covered most of the seeds that they needed to make it through the winter. The coveys had to leave the thick hedgerows that gave them protection against predators to find new food sources. As they struggled through the snow, Cooper's hawks picked them off one by one. Goshawks and bobcats joined in the easy meal plan, and by the time spring came about 90 percent of the local quail population had perished. Of the three hundred quail Daryl and Rob had carefully banded and monitored, only thirty remained.

California quail are clearly not adapted to truly Canadian winters. But since 1969 they have built up their numbers in the Okanagan Valley slowly but surely and have recently enjoyed five years of very mild winters. On that Christmas Bird Count in 1968 we counted 478 quail in Penticton, and the total plunged to 178 in 1969, reflecting the carnage of the New Year's cold snap. By the late 1970s we were seeing over one thousand quail on our count, and in 2004 we tallied a record 4,566. This is one of the highest counts of California quail in the world, second only to an anomalous count in Burns, Oregon, with only ten participants that manages to report over eight thousand quail. Some day I'll make the trek to eastern Oregon in midwinter to see how they do it.

Spring begins for California quail in mid-March when the coveys begin to break up as birds form pairs. I see a lot of chases in early spring, especially between males, as competition for mates heats up. By early May the birds are in pure nesting mode; a walk around my yard elicits a lot of warning calls from males as they alert their mates sitting on hidden nests.

The nests themselves are exceptionally hard to find. They are well hidden, and the females remain sitting until an intruder is literally inches away. Although there are probably three pairs that nest annually in my backyard, I have only found five nests in the last ten years, all quite by accident. I found one while weeding the road bank above my flower beds: I pulled up a large clump of knapweed, and the female rocketed out between my legs. There, in a cup previously covered by the weeds, were fourteen speckled eggs. I carefully replanted the knapweed, and the nest successfully hatched about ten days later. Another nest I found in the fall—this one was hidden in deep pine needles near the creek, and all that was left were the eggshells—each obviously pipped in a nice circle by the hatching chick indicating another successful nest. That nest had twenty-two eggs, near the maximum reported for the species.

The most interesting nest in my yard I found after taking an old rusty table away from my shed wall and setting it out for the garbagemen to take away on April 20, 2004, the designated spring cleanup day that year. Three days later my son noticed seven eggs in a cup of dried leaves that had previously been hidden by the table. I leaned an old wooden toboggan over the nest, hoping the female would keep laying eggs. And keep laying she did.

The following morning I carefully checked the nest and was happy to see it contained nine eggs. Happy, but a bit puzzled—a quail usually lays only one egg per day. I peeked again that afternoon and there were eleven eggs in the nest. Something different was clearly going on. I suspected that more than one female, perhaps three or four, were laying eggs in this nest. These are called dump nests and are a strategy of some females to get other females to raise their young. It often succeeds in species such as ducks, quail, and their relatives, since the young require a minimum amount of mothering attention and no direct feeding.

I kept track of egg numbers daily from then on. The biggest increase in the shortest time was on April 25 when four eggs were laid between 9 AM and 6 PM. By May 1 there were twenty-seven eggs in the nest—the largest clutch ever reported in a California quail nest. We then settled back to see which female would begin incubating the eggs but no volunteer ever stepped forward. It seems that all the females were assuming someone else would do the work of incubation and so the eggs sat unattended for weeks. Eventually I collected them up and donated the clutch to the vertebrate museum at the University of British Columbia.

After collecting the eggs, I replaced the toboggan with a small table similar to the original one I'd thrown away. I forgot to check the site the following April, but on May 30 I found a quail nest with twenty-one eggs tucked under the table. No female ever sat on that clutch either. I think the females must have eventually learned their lesson, because in 2006 none laid any eggs in the nest.

The first young appear around the end of May in my neighborhood—golden-brown fluffballs the size of walnuts running behind their parents. They are easy prey for the neighborhood cats and dogs, and the numbers in each brood steadily decline as the summer progresses. As soon as the first brood has hatched, the female begins to lay a second clutch and may even attempt a third. We often seen small young in early September, but I imagine these birds would have to face winter weather before they are entirely prepared for it.

In late summer the family groups begin coalescing into larger coveys, so I often see groups of thirty or more quail of different ages and sizes foraging on my lawn. As fall turns to winter, the coveys often merge again, forming groups of fifty or a hundred that prowl the neighborhood in set routes, going from garden to garden, feeder to feeder, then returning to their traditional roost site at dusk. Quail like to roost off the ground in dense vegetation; their favorite choices in my district are hedges of columnar cedars. During the day they spend a lot of time hidden in thick brush. Piles of orchard prunings tossed into gulches provide ideal cover for them.

In Canada, California quail have always been tied to rural and suburban habitats at low elevations, but in the last few summers groups have been seen higher in the mountains. As large wildfires clear forests at mid-elevations, quail move up into the rich, brushy habitats that quickly replace the burned forests. They have been moving north as well, surviving in areas that previously had winters too harsh for them. How long they will continue to prosper is anyone's guess, but as long as the climate remains benign and rural plantings prevail, I know I will often see quail scampering across the road with their topknots bobbing. And I am always happy to see them.

CHICKADEES

*I*N LATE DECEMBER 1984 I traveled north to Wells Gray Provincial Park with a group of friends to help inaugurate the local Christmas Bird Count. We had been invited there by Trevor Goward, noted lichenologist and all-round naturalist, who lived at the edge of this magnificent park in central British Columbia. The temperature dropped as we left the relatively balmy coast and snaked through the Fraser Canyon and east across the snow-covered sagebrush benches to Kamloops. By late afternoon we were driving along the North Thompson River, ice swirling in its open reaches, scattered snowflakes drifting down from the afternoon sky. Just before dark we spotted a great gray owl perched on a roadside powerline, listening intently for mice under the snow-blanketed meadow below. With the sighting of that huge northern owl we knew we had entered the depths of a true Canadian winter.

The hospitality inside Trevor's home was warm, and the wood stove kept us toasty, but by late evening the outside temperature had gone below -20°C and I had to venture outside periodically to make sure my aging Volvo was surviving. Living on the coast, I didn't have a block heater that everyone in these parts took for granted, so had to rig up a lightbulb under the blanket-covered hood to keep the engine from freezing.

The following day we toured the park and the upper Clearwater Valley, skiing into Helmcken Falls, one of the most breathtaking sights in the West. There the Murtle River plunges off a basalt cliff in a cascade three times the height of Niagara; in winter a tremendous cone of ice builds from below to add to the amazing scene. By now it was -30°C, and progress was difficult—the snow too cold to slide easily beneath our skis. We had to pole energetically to maintain our speed even going downhill—perhaps fortunate since higher speeds would freeze our tender coastal faces.

I had never been so cold before in my life and had made sure I was wearing full winter gear—long underwear, down jacket, and a scarf over my face to ward off frostbite. Frost crystals formed on my eyebrows and eyelashes. I kept thinking of all the forest animals and how they survived the cold, the moose eating as much willow as they could to slow their inevitable weight loss, the bears fast asleep in cozy dens. And then in front of us a small band of black-capped chickadees appeared in the birches. Tiny birds, the size of my thumb, jauntily flitting along the branches and giving their irrepressible *chik-a-dee-dee-dee!* calls as if they were out on a family picnic. My spirits immediately brightened and complaining thoughts of the cold vanished.

How do these little balls of feathers last more than a few minutes in the cold? First of all, their healthy, plump appearance in frigid weather is largely due to their fluffed-up feathers,

creating a small but important layer of warm air above their skin. In hot weather birds press their feathers close to their body to help lose heat. Secondly, they restrict the blood flowing to their bare feet and legs when the temperature drops. They can tolerate numb toes, since almost all the muscular action needed to move the legs and toes happens in the feathered thigh section; a system of pulley-like tendons operates the strong feet. This adaptation allows chickadees and other birds to drop the temperature of their feet to freezing and still be quite functional.

Most important of all, small birds such as chickadees must eat almost constantly during cold weather to stay alive. Since high-energy food can be hard to find in the depths of a northern winter, chickadees store food throughout the summer and fall. Each little flock maintains a territory in the forest and fills it with cached seeds, hidden in tree bark or clumps of dead leaves. They have a very good spatial memory as to where these caches are and have been shown to find them very easily a month or more after the food is hidden. Some studies have even found that chickadees expand the spatial memory part of their brain in the fall when they are hiding food. So if you notice a chickadee going back and forth to your feeder taking sunflower seeds at a great rate, it is undoubtedly caching them in the woods somewhere, not stuffing its belly.

Like most forest birds that don't migrate south in winter, chickadees travel in small flocks through the day. This behavior helps each individual find food more often and reduces the chance of getting caught by a hawk, since each member of the flock is constantly on the lookout for both food and danger.

Unlike other flocking birds, such as nuthatches and kinglets, chickadees rarely roost together on cold nights to conserve their body heat. Instead, each bird simply finds a tree cavity or clump of thick branches for itself and snuggles inside. They drop their body temperature as well—a short-term hibernation called torpor—to save on heating costs until they have to fly the following morning.

The next day we divided up the Wells Gray area and conducted the bird count. I was used to counts in southern British Columbia where most groups see about forty or fifty species of birds for the day—this time Trevor and I saw only forty-nine birds of eleven species, and we had the best list of the count! But eighteen of those birds were black-capped chickadees, clear evidence of the success of their winter survival strategy. They are also conspicuous little birds, constantly calling to advertise their presence. Although these calls may increase the chances that they will be discovered by a small hawk or pygmy-owl, they are vital to keep the flock together. The *chik-a-dee* call also serves as a predator warning—biologists have discovered that the number of *dee* notes repeated at the end of the call is directly related to the severity of the threat. So if a black-capped chickadee spots an owl in a tree it might give ten or more *dee* calls, but if it's just trying to stay in touch with friends and family it would stick to one or two.

Black-capped chickadees also have a distinctive song—a clearly whistled *fee bee* or *fee bee-bee*, the first note a third above the next ones, which are on the same pitch. This song is a very common part of the woodland soundscape throughout the range of chickadees, but many people don't recognize its source. If you hear those whistled notes, as you often do in the spring and early summer, you can call in the singing bird with a simple imitation of the song. It is essentially a territorial signal, so the calling bird is almost surely a male and will come to see who is trespassing on his land if he hears a reply.

There are four species of chickadees in the mountain forests where I live, and, like most birds, each has its own song and calls. Mountain chickadees add another note into the song, making it *fee fee bee-bee*, the first two notes descending. The other two species, the boreal chickadee and chestnut-backed chickadee, don't give any version of the *fee bee* song but have distinctively nasal *chik-a-dee* calls.

Each species has its own forest type as well. Black-capped chickadees are found mainly in deciduous woods along creeks and lakes and in gardens; mountain chickadees are birds of drier coniferous forests. Boreal chickadees prefer northern and high-elevation spruce forests, whereas chestnut-backed chickadees live in very moist coniferous forests. These habitat differences break down somewhat in winter, and a lucky birder might see all four species in one flock.

All chickadees nest in tree cavities; if the female finds a nice rotten stump she can excavate the cavity with her bills, but she will happily take over a hole made in a previous year by a nuthatch or small woodpecker. The nest is lined with a thick, soft layer of moss and fur. Some chickadees find owl pellets on the ground and rip them apart to supply the fur layer. I was surprised once when checking a nest box by a hissing *khaaaa!* coming from the box, accompanied by a puff of dry mouse fur drifting out of the hole. I gingerly opened the roof of the box and peered in—there was a female mountain chickadee sitting on her eggs, almost buried in the fur and bones of shredded owl pellets. Every few seconds she would open her beak wide and exhale in a surprisingly loud hiss. I have since learned this is called the snake display and is common to all chickadees; it is certainly well named and I'm sure would effectively deter a lot of would-be nest predators.

After the nestlings fledge and become independent, breeding birds form flocks of a half-dozen or so birds that roam a larger area than the breeding territory through fall and winter. The young birds disperse and try to insert themselves as low-status members in one of these flocks, hoping that eventually an older bird will die so that they can move up the social ladder.

As I write this it is late October, and mixed flocks of chickadees, nuthatches, and kinglets roam the woods behind my house throughout the day. Their chatter tells me where they are, so if I ever feel the need for a bit of a mental lift I just have to step outside and watch the flock. I can't think of any other bird that has so much spirit and bright-eyed intelligence stuffed into such a tiny package—it is simply impossible not to feel the infectious enthusiasm for life in a chickadee.

PYGMY NUTHATCH

*A*BOUT ELEVEN YEARS ago I lived with my family in Vancouver. Life was good—I had a great job at the University of British Columbia, and we lived in a wonderful neighborhood in Kitsilano—but something was missing. I had grown up in a place where I could roam the woods pretty much whenever I liked, something that was really not possible in Vancouver. We would go on family walks to see the ducks at Jericho Beach and hike the trails of Pacific Spirit Park, but these events had to involve adults, and our busy lives ensured they didn't happen often.

On one of our frequent visits to my parents' home in the Okanagan Valley, we decided to look for houses in the neighborhood. The first two days didn't turn up anything that would draw us away from the coast, but on the third day the real estate agent showed us a house set on the edge of a creek gully, the narrow watershed filled with big cottonwoods and ponderosa pines. As we got out of the car, a veery gave its gorgeous downward-spiraling song from the chokecherry tangle below. That tune would be nice to wake up to, I thought, as the agent rattled on about the new appliances in the kitchen. Then I heard the piping calls of pygmy nuthatches and looked up to see a line of little fledglings perched on a pine branch, calling to be fed. This place was clearly a good spot to raise a family.

Pygmy nuthatches don't have complicated habitat preferences—they simply love ponderosa pines and are rarely seen more than a short flight from one of the big, orange-barked trees. As their name suggests, they are the smallest of the nuthatches, a family of songbirds that specialize in combing tree bark for insects and other suitable food items. They have the unique ability to crawl both right-side-up and upside-down on tree trunks, so they can look into cracks from every angle. Their sharp bills are rather strong for their size, allowing them to chip off good chunks of wood as well as build cavities in rotten trunks for nesting and roosting.

One characteristic that sets pygmy nuthatches apart from their close cousins is their gregarious nature. You rarely see a single pygmy nuthatch; pygmies travel through the woodlands in loose flocks of ten or more birds. Their constant chatter makes them easy to find amid the pines most of the year as they forage along the branches, looking into the clumps of long green needles and poking into the big cones. These flocks attract birds of other species as well, and most groups include a few red-breasted nuthatches, white-breasted nuthatches, mountain chickadees, brown creepers, golden-crowned kinglets, and often a woodpecker or two. Despite their small size, the pygmy nuthatches are the dominant birds in these flocks, and the other birds follow them through the pines.

These mixed-species flocks are a characteristic feature of coniferous forests, especially in winter. I have walked for an hour or more on Christmas Bird Counts, wondering where all the birds are, then encountered one of these groups. Suddenly the trees are alive with birds, and the only way I can accurately count them is to wait patiently for them to move to another grove. Then I can tally the birds as they follow the leaders from tree to tree, the short-tailed nuthatches easily separated from the long-tailed chickadees.

Flocks of pygmy nuthatches are based on family groups, which stay together year-round. They usually consist of the mother, father, and young of the year, but many family groups also include one or more helpers. These helpers are usually male progeny from the year before helping their fathers, although one was studied helping his brother. They hang out with their father during the second summer of their lives, helping to feed the incubating female and later the brood of young. Most find mates of their own the next year, but a few help out for two years in a row.

Belonging to a flock, especially in winter, has some obvious advantages for nuthatches. Individuals are less likely to be singled out by a predator than if they were traveling alone, and flocks may have an easier time finding good food sources if every member is searching. But at night, another factor comes into play: the cold. On mild nights, pygmy nuthatches will roost in a tree cavity with their family group, all huddled together to stay warm. But as the temperature drops, groups coalesce in the afternoon and roost together. Sometimes more than 150 nuthatches squish into one tree cavity. The ones on the bottom of the pile save the most energy in such an arrangement, but very occasionally can be suffocated by the stack of nuthatches on top of them.

Pygmy nuthatches forage out on branches more than the other nuthatches, which spend most of their time on tree trunks. Pygmies look for insects in the base of pine needle clusters and whack vigorously at bark to see what's underneath. In the late summer and early fall they probe into ponderosa pine cones to remove the big seeds as well. I've seen them sallying out to catch flying ants on the wing, especially when there is a significant hatch of the insects. At those times when food is abundant they cache a lot of what they find, ramming the ants or seeds into cracks in the bark. They retrieve that food later in winter or even later in the day if they get hungry. One pygmy nuthatch was actually seen using a short twig to probe into bark crevices for food, much like the famous woodpecker finches of the Galapagos Islands.

Because they need large snags to nest and roost in and like to forage on the branches of big old pines, pygmy nuthatches are very sensitive to changes in the structure of their pine forest home. Selective logging practices that remove larger trees and snags can cause a rapid 50 percent decline in nuthatch populations. If those practices are repeated at short intervals, creating dense forests of young pines, pygmy nuthatches will disappear completely. The Black Hills of South Dakota were once covered in a healthy ponderosa pine forest filled with pygmy nuthatches, but repeated logging on a ten-year rotation has reduced the population to fewer than a dozen pairs.

There are few bird calls that stir my heart more than the simple piping of the pygmy nuthatch. When I stand on my patio in the morning and listen to the birds the sheer energy in a passing nuthatch flock is a great inspiration for me to get to work. My wife and I even chose a picture of a pygmy nuthatch as the logo of our consulting company. Yes, we bought that house the morning after our visit with the real estate agent and have never regretted the move. Our two children have grown up with bears and great horned owls and nuthatches in their backyard and often played for hours down by the creek with their friends. Both are near fledging themselves now, and I know they will carry that love, knowledge, and respect of nature for the rest of their lives.

WHITE-HEADED WOODPECKER

*L*IKE PYGMY NUTHATCHES, I love ponderosa pines. And it's not just because
the trees are beautiful, their strong branches holding graceful sprays of long needles set off against the rich orange of the
stately trunks. I love the open character of ponderosa woodlands; the sunny, grassy understory draws me into them to
explore one ridge after the other. In spring the bunchgrass is
spangled with the yellow flowers of balsamroot, and in winter
the thin blanket of snow enhances the color of the trees without making walking difficult.

As I walk through the trees I am, of course, always looking
and listening for birds. I hear plenty of nuthatches and chickadees busily searching the trees for insects and other morsels,
and every so often I stop to whistle like a pygmy-owl to see if
one of those little raptors is around. But in the back of my mind
I'm always hoping to see one particular bird, the Holy Grail to
Canadian birders, the white-headed woodpecker. This striking
little woodpecker is highly prized by birders both because of its
rarity and because of its remarkable plumage—a pure white

head set off by a jet black body, a pattern matched by very few birds in the world.

White-headed woodpeckers, like pygmy nuthatches, are closely tied to ponderosa pine forests. They are unusual wood-peckers in that they don't normally feed by excavating holes into dead trees to look for beetles and their larvae. Instead, they spend most of the fall and winter probing ponderosa pine cones to eat the large, nutritious seeds. I remember a friend telling me how he spent all day searching for white-headed woodpeckers near Vaseux Lake but finally gave up and went back to his car to wait for his companions. He was suddenly aware of a gentle rain of pine seeds, or at least the wings off pine seeds, falling on the hood of his car. He looked up toward the sound of a gentle tapping, and there was the object of his search—a little woodpecker out toward the end of a branch, bashing away at the big pine cones.

Pine seeds are so important to white-headed woodpeck-ers that they tend to be rare where there is only one species of big-seeded pine in the local forests. In Washington and British Columbia, ponderosa pine is the only species that fits the bill, but, like most other conifers, it only produces good cone crops every five years or so. White-headed woodpeck-ers are only common in the Cascades of southern Oregon and the Sierra Nevada, where Coulter pine, sugar pine, and Jeffrey pine are added to the mix. With this diversity of big pines, there is a better chance that at least one of the species will pro-vide a bountiful source of winter food for the woodpeckers. Interestingly, the white-headed woodpecker is absent from the extensive ponderosa pine forests on the eastern slopes of the

American Rockies, perhaps because that population of pines has smaller seeds than those farther west.

When I was young my brother Syd and I spent a lot of time hiking through the ponderosa pine forests near Vaseux Lake in the Okanagan Valley. My father was actively promoting the protection of these lands at the time through the Okanagan Similkameen Parks Society. We would go out with him on field trips to show visiting biologists and naturalists the area and felt a growing pride in the special part of the world we lived in. One of the star players in those trips was the white-headed woodpecker. We saw one or more of them every other time we went on a serious hike in the area, a fact at odds with references like *The Birds of Canada,* which listed the species as so rare as not to be a regular member of the Canadian avifauna. I remember the excitement when my father found a nest near Oliver, one of the first ever known in Canada. A couple of years later Syd and I found another nest above Vaseux Lake.

We soon realized that it wasn't just the status of the white-headed woodpecker in the Okanagan Valley that didn't match the information in published references; there were discrepancies between the actual and documented status of several other species as well—the sage thrasher, canyon wren, and white-throated swift for example. All were species typical of the dry intermountain valleys of the American West that entered Canada through the arid lands of the Okanagan. My brothers and I decided to go through our father's notes and write a short journal article reporting on the present distribution of these species. The project quickly mushroomed into a complete book entitled *The Birds of the Okanagan Valley*. And so my modest career in writing was born.

Ironically, as we began to write this book in the 1970s, the numbers of white-headed woodpeckers in Canada dwindled; by the end of the decade we were only seeing about one bird per year. The discovery of a nest in 1981 revived hope that the species was bouncing back, but since then it has remained very rare. The reason for this decline is unclear— the habitat looks much the same as it did ten years before. But perhaps the problem has had a longer timeline. I became involved with conservation planning in the Okanagan Valley with other biologists in the late 1980s, and one of our chief concerns was the state of ponderosa pine forests. One point that was made over and over again was that these forests, though just as extensive as they always had been, had changed considerably in the last century.

Ponderosa pine forests evolved with fire and without logging. For millennia, native peoples burned the dry forest understory every few years, creating a park-like habitat of large, veteran trees and a healthy bunchgrass ground cover. This practice reduced the fuel levels—pine needles, dead branches, and small trees—on the forest floor, lowering the chance that a mid-summer lightning-strike fire would turn into a catastrophic conflagration. It also created ideal habitat for game species and food plants such as balsamroot and spring beauty. The mature pines have a thick bark that protects them from ground fires, so older trees survived and flourished, since the smaller trees and shrubs competing with them for scarce water supplies were eliminated.

When annual burning by native people was banned in the late 1800s and logging companies took out most of the large trees in the first half of the 1900s, the character of the ponderosa pine forests of British Columbia changed completely. Instead of open woodlands dominated by large trees, they became thick forests of young trees. These forests were much less useful for many species of animals that had evolved in the older forests. The large trees produce disproportionately large cone crops, whereas smaller trees bear few cones at all, so seed-eating birds such as white-headed woodpeckers would have been directly affected. Woodpeckers also need large, dead snags to excavate holes for roosting and nesting—these snags are created by fire and felled by loggers, and thus were gone from the new forests as well.

This dramatic shift in the structure of ponderosa pine forests had occurred throughout the West and is now the focus of conservation planning from British Columbia to Arizona. Ecologists in Idaho preparing a state-wide bird conservation plan came up with a single primary goal—to restore half of the extensive ponderosa pine habitat in Idaho to its original open form. Everywhere there is talk of returning fire to western ecosystems, although action is more difficult for obvious reasons—the public is wary of the dangers of wildfire and smoke-filled valleys.

But the cost of inaction is great as well, and not just for white-headed woodpeckers. The fuel build-up in these thick new forests is a recipe for firestorms. In 2003 an August lightning strike touched off a fire in the ponderosa pine forests just north of my home. Within a week it had swept over an entire mountain and destroyed 239 homes on the southern edge of the city of Kelowna. It also destroyed the main powerlines coming into Kelowna, putting extra load onto a small line serving the city from the south. This powerline skirts the eastern shore of Vaseux Lake, and one day the overloaded lines sagged and sparked a second large fire that consumed most of the ponderosa pine forests east of the lake. All those copses I had searched through for white-headed woodpeckers in the 1960s, all the snags I had knocked on looking for nests, were gone within a couple of days. In their place was a charred mountainside that will likely revert to grassland for decades to come. Ironically, a big part of the burned area were two large blocks of land that the Okanagan Similkameen Parks Society had purchased in the 1960s, land that had been set aside to preserve mature ponderosa pine forests.

In the spring of 2003 wildlife biologists had started a habitat restoration program for white-headed woodpeckers at Vaseux Lake. They thinned a small area of forest, then burned the understory in an attempt to recreate the original forest condition. The Vaseux Lake fire raced toward that site in August, a raging inferno burning through the crowns of the trees. But when it reached the restored site it ran out of ground fuel and dropped to the forest floor where it was quickly put out. The biologists, who had been criticized for spending so much money on woodpecker habitat, quickly realized that this incident demonstrated an unforeseen value of their restoration work.

White-headed woodpeckers continue to rank very highly on Canadian birders' "most-wanted" lists. Whenever one is seen regularly in one place the word goes out and people come from far and wide in hopes of seeing this handsome bird. If the fortunes of the woodpecker are directly related to the health of ponderosa pine forests, and it seems very likely they are, it will retain that near-mythical status in Canada for many years to come. Until we have re-created a landscape with scattered big pines covered in cones, this bird will remain a rarity. And while it is, I will always pause on my woodland walks to search out any tapping noise I hear—is that a hungry nuthatch or a white-headed woodpecker?

CALLIOPE HUMMINGBIRD

I GREW UP ON the benchlands west of Penticton, British Columbia. These were not table-flat benchlands like some in the area, formed from the raised deltas of streams flowing into long-vanished glacial lakes. Instead, they were rolling prairies with hollows and hills built of silt and soil that collected at the bottom of the glacial lakes themselves, their surface reflecting the flows of ancestral spring runoffs and huge blocks of ice melting under a blanket of glacial debris. My brothers and I loved exploring these grasslands and knew each dip and bump only too well. The small hollows held snowdrifts on their north-facing sides that made superb toboggan jumps, and the larger ones collected enough water in March to support the growth of wild roses amid the grass. We called one of these the Big Hollow, and it was the site of the most difficult toboggan runs. Its steep sides created record speeds for our aluminum two-seater, but the biggest challenge was to avoid the large rose thicket at the bottom, which was thick enough to stop a flying toboggan in its tracks and catapult the occupants deep into a thorny briar patch.

In spring the roses leafed out, and the grassland bloomed around the Big Hollow—buttercups followed by yellowbells followed by shootingstars. One day in late April or May, we would see another little star at home in the hollow—a male calliope hummingbird. The tiny ball of feathers would be perched on the highest dead rose twig, glancing this way and that, checking for possible mates and potential competitors. His back was emerald green and his throat a blazing magenta starburst of narrow metallic feathers.

Without warning he was off, buzzing high up into the air, then turning and diving straight down toward the ground, pulling up at the last second with an explosive *ptzinngg!* He performed this display for both female and male hummingbirds—a friend even told me of one passionate male that put on a show for a pinecone. But if the object of attention was a female hummingbird he soon switched to another display of aerial talent. Instead of diving down from the height of his climb, he would hover almost motionless, sinking slowly, slowly, toward the roses. This descent ended directly in front of the female where he would raise his purple gorget of throat feathers and make a loud buzzing sound with his wings.

Male hummingbirds, like a lot of tropical bird species that feed on nectar or fruit, take no part in the nesting process other than mating with females. They instead spend the entire breeding season putting on elaborate displays and showing off their impressive plumage. Female hummingbirds tend to be much less colorful, with green backs, speckled throats, and white bellies, and do all the parental chores—building the nest, incubating the eggs, and feeding the young. Male calliope hummingbirds simply find a food source that will attract plenty of females—such as a big patch of roses—then sit back and wait for potential mates to arrive. In areas where nectar flowers are particularly abundant, there can be as many as five females for every territorial male. The males that don't hold a territory at these sites skulk around, waiting for one of the territorial birds to disappear.

Calliope hummingbirds are the smallest birds in North America, weighing 2.5 grams, about the same as five extra-strength aspirins. It would take ten hummingbirds to balance the scales with an adult deer mouse. Despite their small size, calliopes are capable of some remarkable physical feats. They are the smallest long-distance migrant birds in the world, flying a total of 9,000 kilometers each year between their breeding grounds in southwestern Canada and their wintering grounds in western Mexico. I remember birding along a country road in the Sierra Madre Occidental above Mazatlan one sunny day in February, sorting through all the diverse tropical birds when suddenly a calliope hummingbird zoomed into view, sipping nectar from the roadside flowers. I immediately thought of my long flight down to Mazatlan from Canada the day before and how that tiny package of energy had to make the same trip on its own—twice a year for its entire life.

Male calliopes arrive in British Columbia in early April when there are only a few flowers available for nectar. The females arrive a week or so later, by which time the wax currants and other favorite nectar sources are beginning to bloom. Once the female has found a territory and mated with a suitable male, she looks for a good nest site—usually a fairly thick pine branch with another branch right above it to act as an umbrella against the sun and rain. Made of plant down held together with cobwebs, the nest is beautifully camouflaged with a coating of lichen flakes.

The nest looks so much like a simple bump on a branch that the only time I've ever found one is when I've seen the female fly directly to it. And usually that happens when the hummingbird's irascible behavior leads it to attack any living thing that goes near its nest. I've seen hummingbirds buzzing at harmless birds such as chickadees and nuthatches and, knowing that maternal concern could be the only thing driving such behavior, I just sit back and watch until the female gives up on the attack and flies back to her bump-like nest. Hummingbirds are well known for their fearless, pugnacious skirmishes with much larger birds. I've seen big owls perched high in trees, blinking as a small squadron of hummingbirds circled their heads.

The female lays two pure white eggs in the nest, each the size of a small bean seed, and begins to incubate them. Once the young hatch, she busily gathers nectar and small insects for them. Hummingbirds eat a lot of small flies, often stealing them right out of spider webs. Although they are considered nectar-feeding birds, they are probably more accurately thought of as flycatchers with very high energy requirements. So if you worry that the pure sugar-water in your hummingbird feeders isn't providing a well-balanced diet for the birds, remember that they are getting a good variety of flies from your eaves, windowsills, and garden and just need that high-octane sugar to fuel their search for bugs.

Another source of sugar for calliope hummingbirds is the sweet sap of birch and willow trees. The hummingbirds steal this sap from the small holes drilled into the bark by red-naped sapsuckers. The sapsuckers are small woodpeckers that, like the hummingbirds, live on a mix of sugar-water and insects. The wells from which they harvest their sap are also visited by insects, squirrels, and other animals attracted to the natural candy.

Once all the females are sitting on eggs and have stopped reacting to the advances of displaying males, the males drift south, most migrating down the ridges of the Rocky Mountains. There, nectar-filled flowers such as paintbrush fill the alpine meadows, providing an easily available fuel supply for the birds. The females leave as soon as the young are independent, so by late July there are almost no adult calliope hummingbirds left in Canada. The young gain strength on their own, feeding on an abundant supply of small flies and late-blooming flowers, then turn south at summer's end to make the Mexican journey on their own.

And no, hummingbirds do not migrate south on the backs of geese. Although it would be difficult to disprove this fanciful tale outright, the fact that the geese only fly to California instead of Mexico, and do so in October instead of August, makes the prospects highly unlikely for this bit of teamwork.

BLUEBIRDS

*I*N FEBRUARY THE interior grasslands have lost most of their snow but are still seemingly lifeless, the bunchgrass gray-brown and dormant, the pocket mice hibernating in their burrows under the sagebrush and antelope-brush, and the spring songbirds just starting their journeys north from Arizona and California. A walk across the benchlands then can be uncannily quiet and uneventful, punctuated by a few blooming buttercups and the occasional song of an early meadowlark. Then a soft sound comes to your ears, a quiet, ventriloqual twittering. Suddenly you see them—a small flock of birds hopscotching from bush to bush, little pieces of blue sky against the dry grass. The bluebirds are back.

There are two kinds of bluebirds in the southern interior of British Columbia where I live. Mountain bluebird males are brilliant sky-blue, whereas their western bluebird cousins are a deeper, purplish blue and have a rusty breast. The females of both species are duller gray but show bright flashes of blue in their wings and tails when they fly. Mountain bluebirds nest in grasslands and pastures, whereas western bluebirds prefer open woodland—in British Columbia their favorite tree is the ponderosa pine. Neither species is found in thick forests.

Females of both species lay bright blue eggs, appropriately matching their plumage but actually typical for all members of their family—the thrushes. Unlike other thrushes, though, bluebirds nest in cavities, usually old woodpecker holes in trees. This habit provides a lot of protection from nest predators but can severely limit where bluebirds can nest—there aren't many trees out in the grasslands, and fewer still have suitable holes.

Bluebirds likely experienced a bit of a population boom as settlers spread across the West, clearing forests and providing nest sites in outbuildings. Then came nest-site competitors in the form of house sparrows and European starlings; neither species is native to North America, and both are very aggressive when it comes to appropriating real estate. Bluebirds found it harder to find nest sites, and populations probably declined through the mid-1900s.

In 1987 I wrote a book with my brothers entitled *The Birds of the Okanagan Valley* in which we opened the western bluebird account with the following sentence: "Although western bluebirds are usually less numerous than mountain bluebirds in the Okanagan and occupy a much more restricted habitat, they are nevertheless fairly common inhabitants of the Valley." What a difference twenty years makes. There is nothing static in nature, a reality that applies to bluebirds as much as anything. Western bluebirds have greatly increased in number and are now much more abundant and widespread than their mountain cousins in the Okanagan. They are one of the fortunate few species that, for the moment at least, are benefiting from the presence of humans on this planet. Most of the benefit comes from the popularity of bluebird nest-box projects, but there may be less direct benefits as well, even from the booming Canadian wine industry.

For the last three years my son, Russell, my daughter, Julia, and I have banded bluebird nestlings throughout the southern interior of British Columbia. We do it under contract with the Southern Interior Bluebird Trail Society, giving Russell and Julia some summer money and me an excuse to get out of the office and into the field. It's always enlightening when you look carefully at a wild species week after week, year after year, especially when you can individually mark your subjects.

To band the bluebirds, we simply check as many nest boxes as we can during May, June, and July. Members of the Southern Interior Bluebird Trail Society maintain hundreds—perhaps thousands—of nest boxes, so we regularly check the ones that are fairly close to our home base and farther-flung boxes when we can. It's always exciting to carefully open the box and see what's inside—will it be a tightly sitting female bluebird, a brood of young, begging with their yellow mouths agape, a clutch of exquisite swallow eggs set in a feather-lined bowl, or just an empty box? Sometimes we are surprised by a small wasp nest, a sleepy bumblebee, or even the bright eyes and big ears of a mother deer mouse.

If there are young birds—of any kind—we assess them for banding. Until they are five days old or so, the legs of bluebirds are too small to hold the aluminum bands—they slide

off over the tiny feet. Young swallows pose a different problem in that their legs are too fat. All young birds have fleshy
legs that shrink in diameter as the muscles turn to hard sinew
with age. Banding at too early an age for swallows would be
like wearing a ring that is too small for a finger, so we wait
until their legs have shrunk a bit.

Good friends of mine, Al Preston and Margaret Harris,
started banding bluebirds in 1992 and have noticed significant
changes in that time. Their nest boxes are scattered through
the White Lake basin, a big dry bowl of sagebrush, bunchgrass,
and cactus in the south Okanagan Valley. Western bluebirds,
which normally nested only in the open ponderosa pine forests,
have followed the lines of nest boxes out into the sagebrush
grasslands, formerly the sole domain of mountain bluebirds.

And Al and Margaret have had some interesting band
returns as well. One of their mountain bluebird nestlings
showed up the next year as an adult female using a box in Mon-
tana about 500 kilometers west of the Okanagan and on the
other side of the Rocky Mountains. One of the first birds we
found while banding was an adult female bluebird that Al and
Margaret had banded as a nestling three years earlier and about
a kilometer away. So this bird had stuck close to her natal area,
whereas the other bird had not. In 2005 we found two banded
females nesting in adjacent boxes at White Lake. On checking
the band numbers, we found that they were siblings that we
had banded in the next box down the road in 2004.

Although banding provides fascinating information on the
movements of individual birds, the contents of the nest boxes
allow us to easily assess the breeding success of bluebirds. Col-

lecting this kind of information for other species whose nests are challenging to find can be quite difficult, so to be able to count eggs and young simply by peeking in a series of boxes down a country road is a boon to biologists. It is also an activity through which amateur naturalists can, and have, made a big contribution to the knowledge of bird biology.

One such naturalist is Violet Gibbard, a family friend who lives just up the road from me. When I was a boy Violet was the secretary of the British Columbia Nest Records Scheme and provided a model for my brothers and me to follow in carefully recording nesting data. She and her husband, Les, had a large number of nest boxes set up on their twenty-five-acre property and kept scrupulous notes on the boxes' contents through the spring and summer. Western bluebirds made up a big proportion of those nests, and it was the Gibbards' data that allowed us to figure out many of the details of the biology of that species when we wrote our book on Okanagan birds.

Violet's data showed that western bluebirds lay five to six eggs in their first clutch starting in late April or early May, then often lay a second clutch of eggs after the first broods fledge in late June. The second clutch is almost always smaller—usually four or five eggs. Because cavity nests are well protected from predation, success is high—about three-quarters of the eggs laid produce a fledged young. Very few eggs or young are lost to chipmunks, squirrels, and snakes; most of the attrition happens during cold weather when the adults have a hard time finding enough food for themselves let alone a brood of hungry nestlings.

When the autumn frosts remove most insects from the grasslands, the bluebirds begin to drift south in loose flocks. By December all the mountain bluebirds have left Canada for wintering grounds in the southwestern United States and northern Mexico. Many western bluebirds abandon British Columbia for a winter holiday in California, but good numbers stay behind. I find them in groves of Russian olives around the south end of Okanagan Lake, where they share the berries with robins, waxwings, and grosbeaks. Lately they have taken to another food source—grapes. The burgeoning wine industry in the Okanagan Valley has removed habitat for many species that prefer native grassland but has provided food for bluebirds and other berry-eating species. There are always some grapes left on the vines through the winter. Some never ripened properly, and a few were simply missed by the pickers; others are left on the vines purposely—for the icewine harvest. Icewine is such a lucrative product that those grapes are usually netted off to protect them from bluebirds and other berry-loving birds.

The icewine grapes must be picked on the coldest days of winter when the temperature dips below -10°C. Several recent winters have been so mild that some wineries have not been able to complete their icewine harvest. The wintering bluebirds enjoy those balmy days—I have even seen birds investigating nest boxes on sunny afternoons in late December. The number of bluebirds spending the winter in Canada has slowly increased as well—we used to count on a couple of dozen western bluebirds in the Okanagan for our Christmas Bird Counts but now regularly see a hundred or more with the occasional mountain bluebird mixed in.

COMMON POORWILL

*T*HROUGHOUT THE SPRING and summer months, my parents would often take the family on picnics into the hills of southern British Columbia. We would follow the back roads, gravel tracks through the ponderosa pines and sagebrush, and my father would spend the day photographing birds and flowers while my brothers and I looked for nests and caught butterflies in homemade nets. If we were along one of the mountain streams in the area, we would catch grasshoppers in our nets and use them as bait to fish for rainbow trout. At dinnertime my mother would lay out the picnic sandwiches, potato salad, and cold juice from a big thermos.

Some days we wouldn't head for home until dusk, the twilight sky yellow-green behind the dark pines. Lulled by a day in the sun, we quickly nodded off in the back seat until my father shouted, "Poorwill!" Looking up, we could see a pair of bright ruby eyes on the roadside ahead. Dad inched the car forward so that we could all get a look at the small brown bird. Except for the blazing eye-shine, poorwills look for all the world like a pinecone from a distance, colored in shades of brown, gray, and black. If we could, we would stop the car only a few feet from the bird and, leaving the headlights on, all get out to see it at close range. At that distance poorwills are truly beautiful creatures, with pure white throats and silver-spangled backs.

When we got too close (and we almost always did), the bird would fly off like a big moth, flashing its white tail corners as it circled back behind the car to land on the roadside again. And almost always we heard it or another bird give its pure, liquid call: *Poor*-WILL, *Poor*-WILL.

Common poorwills are members of the goatsucker family, close relatives of whip-poor-wills and nighthawks. Goatsuckers (so named because of early beliefs that European species milked goats by night) are related to owls and like them are decidedly nocturnal. Both families have soft, cryptic coloration so that they can remain hidden and undisturbed during the day, but there the similarities end. Goatsuckers have small, weak feet and bills, unlike the heavy talons and hooked beak of the owls. Their eyes are large and reflect light—such as the glare of car headlights—as a bright orange-red glow. This eyeshine comes from a layer of reflective cells behind the retina called the tapetum lucidum. The reflected light gives the retinal cells a second chance to record the light striking it, significantly improving night vision.

But the main adaptation that goatsuckers have for catching insects at night is a huge mouth. Although their bill is small, the gape of their mouth extends back under their eyes so that when it is opened it literally produces an insect trap as big as the bird's head. Special bristles at the corners of the

mouth extend the net even wider. Poorwills hunt from ground perches, looking up with their big eyes to see large insects such as moths and beetles flying overhead, then fly up to catch the insects in their big mouths.

Poorwills nest in the dry valleys of the West, in sagebrush grasslands and open ponderosa pine woodlands. They return from their Mexican wintering grounds in April and leave in mid-September. If the spring weather turns cold after they arrive and insects can't be found, they can survive for days by going into torpor. Torpid birds drop their body temperature to that of the surrounding air and remain in this state of suspended animation until the air warms up once again. Some birds even remain torpid all winter in some sites in California—the only known instance of birds hibernating.

A friend once brought me a poorwill found along the Similkameen River at Princeton in mid-October, fully a month after it should have left for the south. At first I thought it was simply torpid and was somewhat excited at the thought that perhaps birds in Canada occasionally hibernate. It showed definite signs of life, including raising a wing, a classic poorwill defense posture. I inserted a small digital thermometer into its cloaca, but the bird was so cold that the thermometer wouldn't produce a reading. I blew on the bird's breast feathers to see if it was carrying fat in the usual place between the breastbones and saw then why the bird had remained behind instead of migrating. The left collarbone (part of the wishbone familiar to turkey and chicken consumers) was clearly broken, its jagged point pressing against the skin. I made arrangements to get the bird to a wildlife rescue facility, but it unfortunately died that night.

Poorwills become active each night as dusk falls and will remain active until dawn if moonlight provides enough light to see insects by. On a moonless night they will only call for thirty minutes or so until it is very dark. I remember one night I was participating in a Big Day Challenge, trying to see and hear as many bird species as I could in twenty-four hours as part of an annual contest. Our plan had my team starting at low elevations at midnight, then working our way up to the subalpine forests for dawn chorus. I knew poorwills would be hard to find, since there was no moon. We pulled up to one small ranch where I'd heard screech-owls before and got out of the car to listen for them. There was silence until the farm dogs woke to our presence, began to run around, and set off the motion-detector lights. The whole valley lit up (this was one suspicious rancher), and immediately the poorwills began calling as if the full moon had just risen.

Although poorwills are relatively easy to find at night, they are almost impossible to see during the day. Their plumage blends in so well with the pine needles and lichens on the ground that they are essentially invisible. They are loath to fly until you almost step on them; I have only flushed one or two during the day in my entire life. I have seen two nests (both found by someone else) and was surprised at the pure white eggs that stood out sharply against the ground once the incubating bird had flown. The parents do not normally leave the eggs during the day, so the birds rely on their own plumage to hide the nest—well, actually, to hide just the eggs, since they are laid on the bare ground with no pretense of a nest.

We don't know much about most nocturnal animals, and poorwills are no exception. Most of the gravel roads I used to see them on as a child have been paved, and, although poor-wills still call from the hillsides along those roads, they don't sit on the roads anymore, probably a fortunate strategy for them. Whether it is the higher temperature of the pavement or the more frequent traffic that discourages them, I'm not sure. There are still a few gravel roads through sage and pine where I can count on seeing their bright eye-shine in my headlights.

After graduating from high school, I left home to study and work on the British Columbia coast. Twenty-four years later I decided to move back to the Okanagan Valley with my young family. No small part of my decision was to be back in the habitats that I enjoyed when I was young. I remember sitting out on the patio on the first evening at our new home, enjoying some cool drinks after a hard day of moving furniture and emptying boxes. It had been a hot day for early September. I was hoping all the disruption of moving would be worthwhile, that I would be content back in the ponderosa pines. Then, from the hill above our house, a poorwill called. I was indeed content, for as Arthur Cleveland Bent says in his classic work on North American birds, the call of the poorwill, "like the delicious aromatic smell of the sagebrush, clings long to the memory of the lover of the West."

FLAMMULATED OWL

*W*HEN I WAS growing up, there was no
bird so mythically rare in our region as
the flammulated owl. Although we could see its picture in the
Peterson Field Guide and knew that two had been seen within
a twenty-minute drive of our house over the last sixty years,
we never dreamed we would ever find one. Flammulated owls
are tiny owls—weighing only about 60 grams and measuring
about 15 centimeters long. They are grayish-brown, flecked
with salt-and-pepper patterns, and have a row of small flame-
colored feathers on their shoulders that give them their name.
Unlike all other small owls in North America, flammulated
owls have dark eyes. When perched against the trunk of a ponderosa pine tree they are essentially invisible.

They were not only thought of as rare in the Okanagan Valley but also throughout their range in the mountains of western North America. Few people had ever seen
one and almost nothing was known about their biology. The
first record of the owl in Canada had been noted in October
1902, when the renowned bird artist Major Allan Brooks had
found one washed up dead on the Okanagan Lake beach in

Penticton. Another had been shot by a geologist near Kamloops in 1937 as it called near his campsite.

When I was eight years old a logger felled a big old pine tree up the creek from where we lived. The tree was largely hollow and disintegrated on impact with the ground. The faller was surprised to see a small bird flopping about in the wreckage of rust-colored, punky wood. He looked more closely and saw the white shells of several broken eggs. The bird was a small owl with dark eyes. The owl unfortunately died soon after, but I remember seeing it several times in my childhood, immortalized on a picturesque pine branch in the Penticton Museum. My father always remarked about how wonderful it would be to see one alive.

In the mid-1970s my brothers and I began working on a book about the birds of the Okanagan Valley. Part of the research involved leafing through all my father's photographs of birds and local habitats. In one shoebox we came across a remarkable black-and-white print of a juvenile owl perched in my mother's hand. We recognized it immediately as a flammulated—it had the dark eyes, unfeathered toes, and small size; it was literally no bigger than the hand it sat in. We quickly interrogated my father about the bird—he said they had found it in their garage in Summerland in the summer of 1947. He was just beginning to learn his birds at the time and had identified it as a young screech-owl, a common species in the area. He had never even considered flammulated, and like many people put its small size down to the fact that it was obviously a young bird fresh out of the nest. But birds do all their growing in the nest, and once they start to fly, as this one had, they are as big as they are ever going to get.

This find prompted a bit of a campaign in our family to find flammulated owls—surely if one had found its way into my parents' garage they must be commoner than previously thought. We made several trips into the summer nights, but all we had to go on was that the owls seemed to be associated with ponderosa pine forests and they had a quiet hooting call. One trip along Penticton Creek only turned up a close encounter with a big Black Angus bull.

In the summer of 1977 I was working in Shuswap Lake Provincial Park, about three hours' drive north of Penticton. My father wrote to say that he had been corresponding with a California biologist, Jon Winter, who had published a short note reporting that flammulated owls were actually locally common in northern California. To find them, all one had to do was to go out at night to the right habitat and play a recording of their call, then hope an owl would respond. Flammulated owls have a rather low hoot for such a small owl—a soft, ventriloqual *boo*-BOOT repeated endlessly on warm spring nights. If you are not listening for it, you could easily miss it in the soundscape of the mountains with their rushing streams, whispering pines, and jetliners on red-eye flights to Toronto. Jon sent my father a cassette tape with a good recording of the call, and my parents set off into the night to look for owls.

It was early July, so they had to wait until 10 PM to start their search. They spent an hour or so listening up the Shatford Creek valley where the logger had found the nesting bird, but they had no luck. Disappointed, they returned home, but on the spur of the moment decided to try at Max Lake, a little marsh about 3 kilometers behind our house. They got out of the car at the end of the road, began to play the tape, and within seconds heard a response from a flammulated owl. After all those years of mythic rarity, here was a flammulated owl calling in one of our favorite birding areas.

When I heard the news I was just starting a ten-day shift at the park, so it was July 15 before I could get back home to see this owl for myself. My boss, George Sirk, was keen to see it as well, so both of us drove down to Penticton, picked up my parents, and were at Max Lake by dark. I knew it was getting late in the season for owls to be calling; most birds stop acting territorial sometime in the first week of July when they are too busy raising big young to worry about intruders (which is what the tape-recorded call represented to them). We played the tape again and again, but all we heard in the summer dusk were the whistles of poorwills and the hypnotic chirping of crickets.

Then a new sound began from up the hill southwest of the car, a rather menacing, growling hiss: *Khhh! Khhh!* We wondered out loud what it might be; my father suggested a porcupine, my mother thought it was a bobcat. I decided I was going to find out what it was—I was very disappointed in the lack of owls and wanted to get something out of the night. It sounded like it was some distance up the steep mountainside, so I took the big flashlight and began to clamber up the slope. Within seconds I realized it was right above me. I turned the flashlight up, and there, on the lichen-cloaked branch of a big Douglas-fir, was a little gray fluffball with dark eyes—a juvenile flammulated owl.

I called the others up, and we watched for several minutes as the adults came in to feed it moths and beetles. Most owls leave the nest a few days before they can fly well, and flammulated owls are no exception. This one had obviously glided downhill from its nest site. To gain altitude, it would hitch itself up the rough bark of the tree like a little woodpecker, except that it had to use its beak as well as its claws to make any headway. We took some pictures and then, satisfied and elated, retreated back to the car and the comforts of home.

Since they are almost completely insectivorous, flammulated owls are migratory in Canada and the United States. We found that they returned to the Max Lake site in early May each year. We spent the next three years looking in vain for a flammulated owl nest. Like most small owls, they nest in old woodpecker holes, but there seemed to be few available holes around Max Lake, and none had an owl looking out after we knocked. Finally in 1980 my father decided to move a screech-owl nest box from our backyard to Max Lake. I told him he was being overly optimistic but had to eat my words two weeks later when we saw a flammulated owl peering from the box. We carefully monitored the hatching and growth of the two young in this nest, the first flammulated owl nest to be found in a box.

The following year we checked the box in mid-May and found a female looking out. We checked again a week later but no owl appeared. Climbing to the box, we lifted the roof off and looked inside just as a flying squirrel rocketed out of the hole, gliding downslope to another tree. The box had been filled with moss and hair lichens, a typical flying squirrel nest.

Buried under the moss was a dead female flammulated owl, killed by a bite to the back of the head. Two weeks later we found a second nest in a shallow tree cavity only about 100 meters uphill from the box. The male had apparently found a new mate, but unfortunately this rather exposed nest was destroyed by a predator, probably another squirrel. But the year after that the owl was back in the box, and it or other owls nested successfully there for more than a decade.

Flammulated owls are simply one of those creatures that you do not see unless you go looking for them, and you have to go looking in the right place at the right time. Only once have I have seen one away from a nest during the day. One spring I was teaching a field ecology course in the Chiricahua Mountains of southeastern Arizona. After exploring the area for a few days, I was struck by the abundance of owls—whiskered screech-owls were giving their Morse code–like calls from the oaks, elf owls called from the sycamores above my cabin, a couple of pairs of western screech-owls were in the cottonwoods, and at least one flammulated owl was hooting from the highest Apache pines in the valley.

I convinced a pair of students to look more closely at the habitat use by whiskered screech-owls, so we went out for several nights, mapping the location of calling males. We would then go out the following days to take habitat measurements from the calling sites. We drove up to one site, and the students were dismayed to see that the bird had been calling from a steep hillside below the road, thickly overgrown with scrub oak. They pleaded with me to skip this site, but I told them that to be good scientists they couldn't simply ignore data that was difficult to gather. So they bushwhacked through the brush while I birded along the road. Within a few minutes they called out to me, saying I should come down right away. Sensing a plot to get me off the comfortable road and into the tangled branches, I reluctantly descended, but I quickly forgot about my suspicions when the students pointed out a flammulated owl trying to sleep in the middle of the thicket.

Because they are so hard to find when they are not calling or nesting, we know very little about flammulated owls in winter. They presumably migrate to the mountain pine forests of Mexico and northern Central America, where they can be found every month of the year. One biologist even put forward the theory that the flammulated owl might hibernate on its North American breeding grounds, like the poorwill does on occasion, but that idea has been discounted, since there was no evidence that they can hibernate and plenty of evidence that they do migrate.

They seem to leave southern Canada in September and early October as the nights cool down and insect numbers drop. One flammulated owl that was killed hitting a window in Kelowna, B.C., in mid-November had a stomach full of earwigs and a single shrew. The flightless earwigs may have been the only common insect active at that time, and the shrew represents the only record of a flammulated owl eating anything but insects.

Many birders came from all over the country to see the owls at Max Lake. Those from southern British Columbia returned to their homes with a clear memory of the call and a search image for the correct habitat. Rather than the pure ponderosa pine forests we had initially been searching, these birds were in a Douglas-fir forest with only scattered ponderosa pines. A friend of ours from Kamloops soon found that flammulated owls were common in that area, and within a few years the known range of the species had expanded to include the Fraser River north to Williams Lake and all of the Rocky Mountain Trench south of Golden. This was not a real range expansion, of course, but an expansion of knowledge. Research projects from British Columbia to Colorado and Nevada have now gone a long way to demystifying the ecology of the flammulated owl, a species that was not much more than a rumor in the forests of the West three decades ago. Looking back, this little owl has taught me a great deal about how little I know.

NORTHERN SAW-WHET OWL

I REMEMBER ONE MARCH night when I was perhaps twelve years old, getting packed into the car to check out a strange sound reported by a friend of my father's. He said it was a monotonous beeping coming from the mountain above his house, close to an airplane navigation beacon. He thought it was probably a bird, but might be some electric tone coming from a radio in the beacon tower. Since he only heard it at night, he began to suspect it was a small owl. So we drove down to Okanagan Falls to see for ourselves. This trip was a big adventure, since, although we were all keen birders in our family, it was the first time I remember going out after dark to look for an owl.

When we opened the car doors we could hear the sound coming from the steep hillside with scattered trees and the lone red light from the small tower. As the man had said, it was a steady series of short whistles, rather like the sound that big trucks make when they are backing up (though I don't remember that safety feature being a part of the world in the mid-1960s). We hiked up the rocky slope and soon found that the sound was coming from a big Douglas-fir. Whatever was making it stayed hidden, though, until we got too close and a small brown owl the size of a big coffee mug swooped off into the darkness. The whistles immediately started again, this time from another tree.

Looking in our field guide, we knew the bird had to be a saw-whet owl, one of the smaller owls in North America, weighing less than 100 grams. Saw-whet owls are very nocturnal; waking after it is seriously dark, then venturing out to hunt for mice. They are sit-and-wait predators, perching on a branch and listening for mice in the grass below. By day, they roost in thick vegetation. Although they are common—probably the commonest raptorial bird in southern Canada and the northern United States—saw-whet owls are rarely seen. That bird in Okanagan Falls was the first I remember seeing, and I have met several keen birders who have never seen a saw-whet owl.

I was really introduced into the world of saw-whet owls through the flammulated owl. After that pair of flammulated owls nested at Max Lake in 1980 we built about thirty nest boxes and put them up in various parts of the Okanagan Valley in hopes that flammulated owls would fill them. Instead, the next year I found only three of the boxes with owl tenants, and those were all saw-whets. Although I had been set on studying the flammulated owl, I checked the literature and found that, although the saw-whet's winter diet and migration routes were fairly well documented, next to nothing was known about its breeding biology. So in 1984, with the help of friends and family, I put up over two hundred nest boxes in the forests of the south Okanagan. So began a decade of serious work on these small owls, and a lifetime of interest.

Saw-whets, like most owls that eat mice and other mammals, nest early to take advantage of the long nights of late winter and spring when they are feeding their young. Male saw-whet owls begin their monotonous tooting in February or even late January, hoping to attract a female with their far-carrying calls. When an interested female arrives, the male shows her a suitable nest hole, usually a cavity excavated by a northern flicker or pileated woodpecker. The female snuggles into the hole, and thus begins the nesting season.

At first the male catches as many mice as he can and brings them to his new mate. This practice impresses her deeply and also gives her the nutrition needed to lay five to seven eggs. In years when mice are plentiful, the male will bring more than the female could eat; I remember looking into one nest box where a female sat on her eggs surrounded by twenty-one mice. The little rodents were stacked like cordwood and surprisingly sorted to species—the deer mice on one side, the voles on another, and a pile of shrews in behind.

Saw-whets are consummate mousers. They specialize in forest mice, especially the ubiquitous and common deer mouse. Even though the deer mouse is probably the most abundant rodent in southern Canada and the northern United States, the saw-whet owl is the only animal that really keys in on it as a prey item. Being strictly nocturnal, saw-whet owls hunt entirely by sound. Their large head is predominantly taken up by a pair of remarkable ears. If you look at the skull of a saw-whet, you'll see that the right ear is large, round, and pointed upward, whereas the left ear is much narrower and pointed downward. This asymmetry—found in only a few species of owls—allows the birds to know exactly where a mouse is in three-dimensional space based only on the sound of the leaves rustling under its tiny feet. Most other animals (including us) can only get a vague left-right sense of where a sound is coming from and would have to see the mouse to catch it.

Owls have a strict division of labor during the breeding season: the female incubates the eggs and broods the young while the male provides the food. Once the full clutch of eggs is laid (and copulation stops), the male brings the female far fewer mice—usually only one per night. If mice are easily found, he may fly to the other side of his territory and begin tooting again, hoping to attract a second female. I have found bigamous males three times, each feeding young in two nests several hundred meters apart. A colleague in Idaho once found a male trying to feed two nests with young and a third incubating female, but he couldn't keep up. He stopped feeding the third female, and she abandoned the nest.

Female saw-whet owls also can have two mates in one season. When the young are about three weeks of age and can keep themselves warm, females stop brooding them and either begin helping the male with feeding chores or simply leave. The ones that leave often look for a second mate and raise another brood in midsummer.

I was once trying to net and band an unmated male saw-whet owl in the birch woodlands along the Okanagan River north of Osoyoos Lake. He had been singing heartily for a week, only a stone's throw away from an active nest where another pair was feeding young. I set up a mist-net in a clearing and put up a model owl on a post in front of the net. I then settled back into the bushes and began whistling like a male saw-whet while trying to ignore the clouds of mosquitoes. The unmated male completely ignored my whistling and kept up his own serenade, perhaps not surprising since he was trying to attract a female, not attack another male. After a half-hour, I gave in to the mosquitoes and got up to take down the net when I was surprised to see an owl in it. The male was still calling—who was this? I pulled the bird out of the net, checked the band, and recognized her immediately as the female from a nest about 2 kilometers to the north. She had left that nest a few days before and was obviously checking out the bachelors in the area. She never did hook up with the male at that site, though, perhaps put off by the indignity of being netted in the middle of her girls' night out.

While the female is brooding the young, she keeps the nest surprisingly clean, considering the number of dead mice being consumed and the amount of waste produced. But once she stops brooding, the nest quickly becomes a rather putrid mass of fur, bones, guano, and rotting mice. By the time the young leave at about five weeks of age, there are often 10 centimeters of malodorous material caked into the nest cavity. It's not surprising to find out that a saw-whet pair never uses the same nest cavity twice. But this material is gold to a biologist like myself, containing evidence of everything the young have been fed for the last two weeks of the nesting period.

In any given nest, young saw-whet owls are of remarkably different sizes. This is because owls begin incubating eggs as soon as they are laid, instead of waiting until the full clutch is laid as most birds do. Since eggs are laid one at a time every two days, a standard clutch of six eggs is laid over a ten-day period. After a twenty-seven-day incubation period, the young begin hatching over the same range of days, so the first egg laid hatches ten days before the last one. The oldest and largest young can always get food when he is hungry by shouldering out his smaller siblings, and the youngest nestlings are only fed when their siblings are satiated. So if mice are hard to come by, only four or five nestlings from a brood of six will survive to fledging. But if mice are plentiful they all survive. Indeed, if the oldest nestling is feeling well-fed, it will often take a mouse that the adult male has brought in and tear it into bits, offering the morsels to its hungrier nest-mates as its mother did when she was brooding them.

Most owls in North America are relatively sedentary, remaining on their territories with their mates year-round. Saw-whet owls are much more nomadic, and many of them migrate out of their northern breeding grounds for more temperate winter habitats. These migrations are especially noticeable around the Great Lakes, where hundreds of birds are occasionally seen roosting in thickets along the north shores of the lakes in October, waiting for weather suitable for crossing the watery expanse. They are easily banded at this time, and many studies have shown that they move from southern Ontario to New Jersey and beyond.

A similar movement has recently been discovered through southwestern British Columbia; owl enthusiasts have banded over four hundred saw-whet owls each fall at Rocky Point at the south end of Vancouver Island. There the owls gather before crossing the broad waters of Juan de Fuca Strait. However, there is one place in North America where saw-whets are completely nonmigratory: the Queen Charlotte Islands.

The Queen Charlottes lie about 100 kilometers off the north coast of British Columbia, separated from the mainland by the treacherous waters of Hecate Strait. The islands are a dark green archipelago of rain forest with unique flora and fauna that have been separated from continental life since the glaciers retreated 10,000 years ago. The saw-whet owls on the islands are distinctly different from their mainland cousins—where the continental birds are white, the island birds are a rich buff. Their calls are similar, though the island owls' calls are a bit higher pitched. They are considered a distinct subspecies, *Aegolius acadicus brooksi*, named after the famous bird collector and illustrator, Major Allan Brooks.

In April 1987 I traveled to the Charlottes to see these island owls for myself. The ferry crossing was an adventure in itself: we hit gale-force winds as soon as we left the shelter of Porcher Island and entered Hecate Strait. The shallow waters of the strait are famous for their waves when pushed by high winds, and big green curlers were soon smashing into the restaurant windows on the upper deck. My wife and I spent the nine hours protecting our newborn son from flying chairs and catapulting garbage cans. We land-dwelling people wondered if enduring this turbulence was all in a day's work for island folk, but from the talk on the Charlottes over the next few days it was clear this April storm had been a strong one.

We spent the next week on the islands, camping from Tow Hill in the north to Copper Bay in the south. I found thirteen saw-whets calling; twelve of them were in remnant patches of old-growth forest. There were several singing in the lush riparian forests along the Yakoun River around the famous (and then still-standing) Golden Spruce, and even the strip of big Sitka spruces along the beach at Copper Bay was enough to attract a couple of calling males. But the vast clear-cuts and stands of thick second-growth timber in the center of Graham Island seemed all but empty of owls.

Although saw-whet owls can be found in almost any kind of forest, from birch woodlands along creeks in sagebrush deserts to subalpine forests of spruce, they need two things. The first is a supply of large dead trees that will attract wood-peckers to excavate cavities necessary for the owls' nests. The second is an openness to the forest that promotes a diverse understory, resulting in plenty of mice and the opportunity to easily hunt them. Second-growth forests, between about twenty and a hundred years of age, provide neither of these characteristics in any quantity, and modern harvest plans call for logging these forests before they become suitable. Even with the presence of a large protected area on the Queen Charlotte Islands, the projected habitat losses through forest harvest were considered serious enough that the endemic sub-species of saw-whet owl was listed as threatened in 2006.

Slow habitat loss is likely occurring on the mainland as well, but the saw-whet owl population is still large enough that we haven't noticed any dramatic change in their popula-tion. But we don't monitor owl populations well enough to know. We should go out more at night and get to know them on their home turf; otherwise they may quietly disappear while we sleep.

NORTHERN PYGMY-OWL

*M*Y FATHER TAUGHT me many things in life, but one of the most useful tricks he passed on was how to whistle like a pygmy-owl. The clear, measured whistles acted like magic on a quiet winter forest. Where there had been only the sigh of pines over a blanket of snow there quickly developed an animated scene filled with frenetic chickadees calling, jays screaming, flocks of crossbills circling, nuthatches flying in from all around, and, with any luck, a pygmy-owl calling back like a belated echo.

This trick was true birders' lore. Dad said he learned it from Eric Tait, an orchardist and part-time bird biologist from my mother's hometown of Summerland. Eric in turn had picked it up on field trips with Major Allan Brooks, one of North America's best-known bird artists and collectors of the early twentieth century. Brooks told colleagues that he had learned the pygmy-owl effect from his father, William E. Brooks, who had been a civil engineer in India. Like his son, the senior Brooks was an avid bird collector and often employed locals to help him find rare birds in the Indian forests. One of them called like a pygmy-owl to draw out the songbirds, and William used the technique for the rest of his time in India. When the family immigrated to Ontario, William was disappointed that there were no pygmy-owls there and that the whistles had no effect on local birds. But when Allan moved to British Columbia in 1897, he quickly learned the call of the northern pygmy-owl and used it constantly while in the field.

Brooks was always proud to show off his pygmy-owl skills to fellow ornithologists. When Percy Taverner, the curator of the National Museum in Ottawa, came out to the Okanagan Valley in 1922, Brooks confidently predicted that he could call in pygmy-owls at will, but, as Taverner says in his report on that trip:

> We called this call something like a million times with varied but sometimes remarkable success. However, we never heard an answering call. Brooks tells us that last fall when he was demonstrating it to Swarth [a professor from Berkeley] at Okanagan Landing, two owls came to it embraced in a vicious fight and came tumbling to earth... Swarth was rattled and missed them both.

Why do pygmy-owl whistles, simple *kook* notes repeated every two seconds or so, have such an effect on neighboring birds? The answer lies in the biology of the owls themselves and in some surprising twists of bird behavior. Pygmy-owls are diurnal birds; that is, they are active during the day and sleep at night, unlike their nocturnal relatives. They hunt mice, especially voles, which are active both day and night, but also prey

on birds when the opportunity arises. The other forest birds, therefore, recognize pygmy-owls as enemies.

You wouldn't intuitively think that birds should be attracted to the calls of their enemies. When a chickadee hears a pygmy-owl, the logical course of action would be to find a thick shrub and hide until the calling stopped. But instead the small birds fly toward the sound, calling loudly themselves. They join a growing band of birds around the owl in a behavior called mobbing. Several theories have been put forward on the benefits of mobbing, but two seem to answer the question best. Firstly, pygmy-owls and other predators catch most of their prey by surprise. So, if the chickadees and other small birds can find the calling owl, they can watch its movements and flee when necessary. Secondly, by giving alarm calls, the small birds can notify all the other potential prey species in the area of the owl's presence. Once the owl realizes that it won't be surprising anything in this part of its territory, it will presumably fly off to try its luck elsewhere.

Although birds have innate responses to predators' appearances, like the shape of a flying hawk or the round face of a large owl, they must learn the calls of their enemies. So if you imitate a pygmy-owl in a forest where there are no pygmy-owls, no birds will respond. A strong response from chickadees and other forest birds tells you that you are almost surely in an active pygmy-owl territory.

Pygmy-owls are, as their name suggests, very small owls. Weighing only about 50 or 60 grams, they are between a sparrow and a robin in size. They lack the big, round face of other owls, perhaps not surprising since this facial disk is the external ear of owls. Since pygmy-owls hunt visually, they don't really need the sensitive hearing typical of the family. The other curious feature of their plumage is the presence of two dark spots on the back of their head. These spots look remarkably like eyes from a distance. They are obviously meant to fool other birds into thinking that the owl is looking at them when it is not, but why would that deception be an advantage? At least one other unrelated bird shares this pattern of false eye-spots—the kestrel—so it seems to be a trait of small predators. The theory that seems to fit best is that the eye-spots are directed at mobbing birds, perhaps keeping them from making serious attacks from behind that could injure the owl.

Although mobbing is on balance a good strategy for the mobbers, it does occasionally backfire. I was showing a group of university students the effects of imitating a pygmy-owl call in the hills above Vaseux Lake in the south Okanagan when a flock of pine siskins flew in to investigate the sound. They flew excitedly around our heads, searching frantically for the owl they thought had to be there. Suddenly there was a rush of small wings, and a pygmy-owl was sitting on the branch right in front of us, clutching a siskin. I still feel a bit of remorse about that incident; I had unwittingly made the siskin drop its guard while attracting a predator at the same time.

Northern pygmy-owls are fierce killers for their size; they will often try to catch birds bigger than they are. Starlings and robins are common targets, and I've even heard of one capturing a California quail. Like falcons, they have unusually long toes and very sharp talons, both features designed to hold birds in a tight grip. Occasionally their strategy of attacking larger birds gets them into trouble.

My friends Al Preston and Margaret Harris were hiking along a spring-fed creek one bitterly cold winter day when they saw a strange shape in a shrub next to the cattails. On closer inspection they realized it was a pygmy-owl, literally frozen to the bush in a block of ice that enclosed its wings, legs, and tail. Looking around for clues to how the owl got in this predicament, they saw tracks of a Virginia rail—a marsh bird a little bigger than the owl—on the ice between the cattails. These tracks led to a patch of open water where there were feather marks in the snow and signs of a pygmy-owl-sized bird hauling itself out of the water. The owl had obviously tried to catch the rail but had missed and ended up in the water. Thoroughly soaked, it managed to fly to the bush before its water-filled feathers froze solid.

Al and Margaret broke the ice off enough to free the bird, which slowly opened one eyelid to show that it was still alive, though barely. Al slipped the owl into one of his gloves, and they brought the bird over to my house. We melted the rest of the ice off its feathers and forced some warm chicken soup down its throat. The bird opened both eyes as the soup began to do its magic, so we placed it in a shoebox and put that in a dark room, hoping it would continue to recover. An hour or so later I heard a great racket in the backyard— jays and magpies were leading a mobbing gang of some sort. Thinking they had rediscovered a screech-owl we had seen a couple of days ago, I went outside to investigate. I found the birds all gathered around the window of the bedroom, mobbing a pygmy-owl that was perched on the inside win-dowsill, its yellow eyes blazing with contempt. Since the bird was clearly fit for release, we let it go outside and it flew off to the hills.

I'm sure my father had few regrets when he died a few years ago, but one of them was that he had never found the nest of a northern pygmy-owl. I have never found one either, though both of us have spent years knocking on snags with suit-able woodpecker holes the owls would use. I can only assume that they don't peer out of the hole when something taps at the entrance, since the cavities they choose are too small to let in a predator too big for them to handle. But I will keep look-ing and now have a son who will be searching as well. And he knows how to whistle like a pygmy-owl, too.

NORTHERN FLICKER

*A*BOUT FOUR TIMES each year I take part in a radio phone-in program in which I try to answer listeners' questions about birds. The questions range from "What was that little gray bird stuck in my screen door?" to "Can you identify this bird song if I play it on the piano?" to "How can I encourage the neighborhood crows to stop waking me up in the morning with their infernal cawing?" Some of the identification problems can be a bit tricky when creative callers describe a violet-green swallow as "a big green hummingbird with a white face like an owl" or a turkey vulture as a "copper-headed crow."

Over the years certain patterns in the questions become evident, since some common birds seem to catch the public's attention more often than others. Swainson's thrushes taunt backyard birders with their exquisite spiraling songs on summer evenings; the listeners, field guides in hand, wait in vain for the birds to emerge from the forest thickets to be identified. Anna's hummingbirds sip nectar from feeders in December, causing concerned citizens to worry that they have lured the birds to halt their normal migration by offering unnatural food; I reassure them that these birds are naturally nonmigratory and need that sugar to survive even a mild Canadian winter. But the bird that pops up most often in the radio questions is the northern flicker.

The first thing that attracts your attention to flickers is their unusual appearance—it's often hard to figure out even what bird family they might belong to. If you saw one entering its nest cavity in a tree or heard it drumming on your chimney flashing, you'd guess correctly that it was a woodpecker, but more often than not flickers are doing very unwoodpeckerlike things. They spend a lot of time on the ground, probing the grass with their long, strong beaks, looking for ants. In fall and winter they feed primarily on fruit, gobbling up mountain-ash berries or taking advantage of windfall apples. Flickers often perch sideways on branches, again breaking all the woodpecker rules, and embarrassed birders know them as a species that can take on the appearance of others—is that a robin? A starling? A nutcracker? Oh, it's a flicker.

And though most woodpeckers are primly dressed in patterns of black and white, flickers have a relatively wild plumage. Their brown and gray body plumage is unusual in North American woodpeckers and that plumage explodes into yellow or red wings and tail when they take off, as well as a big white rump.

Because of their predilection for feeding on the ground, flickers migrate out of their northern breeding grounds in winter to find areas with warmer temperatures and less snow. I see them everywhere in September in southern British

Columbia, easily identified by their bounding flight (another habit that ties them to the woodpeckers) and salmon-colored wings. As winter settles in, they congregate in good feeding areas; in my neighborhood that means groves of Russian olive trees or apple orchards.

Some people wait for swallows to return, others listen for robin song, but I know spring is here by the ringing *wicka-wicka-wicka* of territorial flickers. With the first warm days of March both sexes of flickers give this call to attract mates and advertise territory, although it is most often produced by single males. If two members of the same sex meet at a territorial boundary during the breeding season, a fascinating dance ensues. The birds hold their bills tilted upward, swaying back and forth in a mock fencing duel while flicking their wings open to show off the bright colors underneath.

It is in spring that flickers act most like woodpeckers, and it is through these actions that many non-birders encounter them. This is when flickers drum to advertise territory and excavate nest holes in dead wood. The drumming often begins at the crack of dawn, ringing out through the house and shaking the windows as a flicker announces to the world its claim of this territory. Although this sound is treated with respect by other flickers, many humans find it annoying to be woken up with a drum-roll reveille. The flickers, of course, have chosen the house because they have found that the flashing at the base of the chimney or some other structure provides the loudest noise in their territory.

Owners of cedar or log homes can have an even more troublesome problem with flickers—a pair may decide that the house is an ideal site for a nest cavity. The flickers proceed to drill a large hole in the outside wall, then raise a family of noisy young within. The birds aren't easily dissuaded from such a hormone-driven task, either—often the best solution is to offer the pair a ready-built home in the form of a nest box attached to a nearby tree or the house itself.

I often find flickers nesting in the nest boxes I put up in open forests for small owls. Although most woodpeckers have an innate need to excavate a cavity in a tree as part of the breeding cycle, flickers are either lazy or practical enough to recognize a free home when they see one. The only thing they don't like about the nest boxes is the layer of woodchips or sawdust I put in the bottom so that the owls—which don't make a nest of their own—have a comfortable floor to lay their eggs on. Flickers still have the woodpecker urge to clean chips out of a cavity, so they empty the box right down to the bare plywood, then lay their pure white eggs on the floor. Of course every time the incubating bird leaves the box the eggs roll to one corner or the other.

The fact that flickers like my owl nest boxes is not so surprising, since the boxes are designed to mimic flicker nest holes. Because flickers are often the commonest woodpecker in any given woodland, their holes are considered very desirable real estate by many forest creatures, from flying squirrels and packrats to owls, bluebirds, and bumblebees. Nesting in a popular spot can be trying for the flickers if a member of a more aggressive species such as a starling decides it wants your home. I was visiting my parents once when I heard screams coming from a nest box in their garden. I knew that a pair of flickers was in residence but the calls sounded like no flicker I'd ever heard. I grabbed a ladder and looked in the box to find a starling with a choke hold on a flicker. Even though the starling was the smaller of the two, its intense attitude had given it the upper hand in this battle. Trying to rectify the situation, I grabbed the starling, pried it off the flicker's neck, and flung it out of the box. The flicker flew off, and neither bird ever returned to the box.

Flickers actually use the fact that bees often take over their nest sites to their own advantage. Nestling flickers have a startling humming buzz so that when six or more of them are calling at once it sounds like the cavity is filled with angry bees. Biologists believe this noise functions as a strong deterrent to common nest predators such as squirrels that would otherwise happily sneak into the hole and consume the eggs or nestlings.

What I find most interesting about flickers, however, is not their food habits, calls, or importance as forest home-builders—it is the geographical patterns in their plumage and the evolutionary stories they tell. In eastern North America, flickers have bright yellow wings and tails, black whiskers, and a red patch on the nape; these are known as yellow-shafted flickers. But from the eastern slopes of the Rocky Mountains west to the Pacific and north to central British Columbia, flickers have salmon-colored wings and tails, red whiskers, and no nape patch at all and are known as red-shafted flickers. Along a narrow band of country in the rain shadow of the Rockies, both forms interbreed and produce a remarkable array of intermediate plumages, ranging from red-shafted flickers with a red nape patch to birds with a red whisker on the left side of their face and a black whisker on the right, to birds with yellow-orange wings, and every other possible mixed-up combination. The two forms look so different that scientists considered them a separate species for many years, but since they interbreed so often wherever they meet they are now considered to be a single species.

Scientists believe that the two forms once looked the same but were isolated during the Pleistocene ice ages into the southeastern and southwestern corners of what is now the United States. Divided by the Great Plains, they became progressively more and more different as the Pleistocene continued. As the thin Laurentide ice sheet melted northward in eastern North America, flickers recolonized the woodlands that formed in its wake. The ice sheet covering the mountains and valleys of southwestern Canada was much thicker and took longer to melt, so by the time the red-shafted flickers moved north from California to southern British Columbia, yellow-shafted flickers had already moved into the plateaus of northern British Columbia. The divide between the two—where intergrade forms are now produced—thus traces a line east of the Rockies north to central British Columbia, then swings sharply westward to the Pacific.

Recent studies within this contact zone on the Chilcotin Plateau of British Columbia suggest that flickers there prefer to mate with birds of their own kind—red with red, yellow with yellow. Time will tell whether this evidence will be enough to convince scientists to split the species in two again, but in the meantime I try to get a good look at every flicker I see to assess its parentage. Almost all the flickers I see in winter have red wings and tails, but a good percentage have traces of red on their nape and black in their whiskers, suggesting that they were born on the plateaus of central British Columbia. The pure yellow-shafted birds of the Yukon and Alaska must migrate east of the Rockies, retracing the path their ancestors took while following the melting ice sheets northward.

So if you are awoken at an ungodly hour by a machine-gun like sound from your roof, relax and try to get a good look at the perpetrator. The color of its wings, tail, and whiskers could tell you a lot about the deep history of our continent.

CLARK'S NUTCRACKER

*M*Y FIRST REAL job (I'm not counting picking apricots and cherries) was working as a naturalist in Manning Provincial Park. Manning was one of my favorite places even before I got the job, a vast area of mountain forests and meadows at the north end of the Cascade Range. Our family often stopped there to picnic or camp on our trips to the coast, and occasionally I had hiked through the glorious alpine flowers toward the Three Brothers. Now I would be working there.

I ended up spending three summers in Manning Park, summers that had a lasting impact on the course of my life. Memories of those days, almost visceral feelings, slip easily into my mind—hiking for hours through hot, aromatic pine forests to finally break out into the open alpine meadows, smelling the fragrant aroma of forest-fire smoke on an August afternoon, staring off at range upon range upon range of blue mountains fading into the hazy distance.

It was in Manning Park that I fell in love with mountains. Although Manning's peaks are low by British Columbia standards, they do have rocky summits with permanent snow-fields, and their flower meadows are legendary. The views from the top are breathtaking—the rock and ice of the Cascades to the south and the dark green, flat horizon of the Thompson Plateau to the north. I would snooze on the summits, luxuriating between the sun-warmed rocks, crusty with dried lichen against my bare legs and arms, drinking in the cold, clear air.

There were few birds on those mountaintops—over the wind I might hear the thin song of the horned larks overhead, the croak of a distant raven, or, with great luck, the soft clucking of a ptarmigan in the rocks. But if I was anywhere near treeline, and on Manning's mountains one always is, I would eventually hear the nasal cawing of a Clark's nutcracker.

Among the most intelligent of birds, nutcrackers are members of the crow family with an exceptional dietary restriction. When the opportunity presents itself, nutcrackers feed like other members of their family, eating carrion and insects, even stealing eggs and young birds from other nests to feed themselves and their fledglings. But in summer and fall they put their strong bills and sharp brains to work on a remarkable harvest.

Whitebark pine is a distinctive member of the treeline community. Its smooth, grayish bark sets it apart from the only other high-elevation pine in the area, the lodgepole pine. But its cones and seeds are what attract nutcrackers. Most pine cones are designed to deter animals from eating the nutritious seeds within, armed with heavy spines or thick pitch. Whitebark cones, in contrast, are rather large, dark purplish, and totally undefended. The mature cones do not open as other cones do, and the seeds would go nowhere but down even if they were released from the cone. The seeds are large and heavy and lack the broad wing typical of other conifer seeds. Whereas the winged seeds of other pines are carried on the wind, whitebark pine seeds are carried in the gullets of Clark's nutcrackers.

Growing at treeline is, by definition, a tough business. Summers are short—usually too short to allow tree germination. On north-facing slopes and in cold hollows the snow lingers late in the summer, cutting the effective growth period even further. Treeline is a place where careful placement of your seeds can be a good strategy for trees, and the whitebark pine has evolved a system that does just that.

In midsummer, when the meadows are a blaze of color with red paintbrush, yellow arnica, and blue lupine, the nutcrackers begin to pry open the whitebark pine cones to eat the unripe pine seeds. They simply eat these unripe seeds on the spot, but as summer turns to an early fall in mid-August, the seeds ripen and the nutcrackers begin to seriously harvest them. Small flocks roam the ridge tops, and the air is filled with the sound of bills whacking against cones. As a nutcracker pulls a seed out of the cone it tests the seed's soundness by clacking it in its bill several times; if the seed is heavy and ripe enough, the bird tosses back its head and stores the seed in a special pouch underneath its tongue.

Once that pouch is full—perhaps with as many as a hundred seeds—the nutcracker flies off to cache the seeds in a suitable place. What the birds are looking for is a site where snow accumulation is light and snowmelt is early; south-facing slopes with sandy soil are ideal. These sites can be right beside the harvest tree or as much as 10 kilometers away. There, the bird digs a shallow trench with its bill, drops a half-dozen seeds into it, then closes the trench again with another swipe of the bill. Throughout the fall, as the larches turn gold and occasional snow flurries dust the ridges, the nutcrackers methodically gather as many seeds as they can, filling cache after cache. In a normal year, each individual may store 30,000 seeds; during a bumper cone crop that figure may be as high as 100,000 seeds.

Except for the wind, winter is a quiet time at treeline. Most of the songbirds have left long ago for their tropical homes in the forests of southern Mexico and beyond. The few birds that remain quietly eat what food they can find, almost all of it stored. The gray jays search out the peanuts they hid after panhandling the food from hikers in July; the chickadees look for ants they crammed into bark crevices in August. Woodpeckers gobble up beetles they find in rotting tree trunks, and spruce grouse sit in their favorite trees eating needles. And the nutcrackers hang around their cache sites, periodically swooping to the ground, brushing away the snow, and coming up with a beakful of pine seeds.

How do they find those caches? Nutcrackers have incredible spatial memory skills; in fact they have outperformed humans in tests where both species had to relocate items they had hidden. Subtle clues on the ground—the placement of a cone or a distinctive rock—are locked away in nutcracker brains during the fall caching season until needed to get breakfast on a cold morning in late January.

In early spring I always saw nutcrackers on south-facing slopes at high elevations in Manning Park. A favorite spot was the Dry Ridge Trail, a short walk through open pine woodlands above the Cascade Lookout. As its name suggests, this trail becomes snow-free relatively early in spring and by summer is almost semi-arid. We naturalists liked to hike it in late May and June, in part because it was the only trail that was snow-free above the valley bottom, but also because of the unusual plants that grew there, adapted to the scarcity of groundwater. There were whitebark pines on the ridge, of course, since the ridge faced south, and the soil there was perfect for nutcracker seed caches.

Although nutcrackers are experts in finding seed caches, they don't usually need to find every last cache to get through the winter and spring, especially after a bumper seed crop the year before. So every spring, as the snow melts and moistens the ground, clumps of whitebark pine seedlings emerge from the gravelly soils, revealing the sites of unused nutcracker caches. Over the millennia, pine and nutcracker have fine-tuned their relationship, the pine producing large, wingless seeds to lure the birds to harvest and hoarding the seeds within their cones until the nutcrackers arrive. The nutcrackers in turn have become entirely dependent on the pine seeds to make it through the year, dutifully planting the seeds in ideal sites for pine germination. In fact, the pines have become adapted to these high, dry sites in part because that's where their seeds were planted by the nutcrackers.

I still drive through Manning Park regularly on the way to the coast, stopping all too infrequently to enjoy the mountains, forests, and meadows. But one change that is hard to miss on a quick visit these days is the tapestry of rust-red trees from one end of the park to the other. The lodgepole pine forests of the valleys and mountainsides are being attacked on a huge scale by the mountain pine beetle. Since these are mature forests— some trees are over two hundred years old—and lodgepole pines are adapted as a pioneer species, I view this development as a natural process that will allow the younger spruce and fir trees growing underneath the pine canopy to flourish and form the climax forest.

But what worries me is the scale and probable cause of this widespread infestation. A seemingly unstoppable period of global warming has produced short, warm winters and long, hot summers, an ideal climate for beetle reproduction and survival. Under these conditions, the mountain pine bee- tle attacks other pines—the ponderosas in lower, hot valleys and the whitebark pines on the mountaintops—in a significant way. In parts of the Rocky Mountains, beetles have destroyed large areas of whitebark pine and with it the interdependent nutcracker–pine system.

Whitebark pines have another insidious enemy as well: the white pine blister rust. This fungus, introduced to the port of Vancouver almost a century ago in a shipment of Euro- pean white pine nursery trees, attacks mature western white pines. This magnificent tree of low-elevation rain forests lost about 80 percent of its population throughout western North America in the first half of the twentieth century. But, like the beetles, the rust can attack whitebark pine and other moun- taintop pines such as limber and bristlecone. Again, some whitebark pine stands in the central Rocky Mountains have been decimated.

As I hike the Heather Trail to the Three Brothers with my children today, the air is still sweet with the smell of valerian in late summer, and sooty grouse still lurk in the dark clumps of fir. The stands of whitebark pine along the trail are still healthy, and we still hear noisy groups of nutcrackers flying to their harvesting grounds. But as I walk, I wonder how long it will take for our deeds—and misdeeds—in the valleys below to weaken the fabric of life here on the mountaintops. That fabric took thousands of years to weave but could unravel within a few decades unless we watch the pines, listen to the nutcrackers, and change our lives accordingly.

CROWS

WHEN I WAS an undergraduate at the University of British Columbia, I lived with my brother Syd in a basement suite in the Locarno Beach neighborhood of Vancouver. It was a reasonable place for a student—although the landlady enjoyed action adventure television programs and was deaf enough to need the volume turned up to maximum. Curiously, she had the ability to hear a female voice in the basement even when all doors were closed. Getting groceries and doing the laundry was also a bit of an expedition, since both were ten blocks away up a very steep hill. But we were close to the university and right next to Spanish Banks, a huge expanse of beach and sandy tidal flats that were essentially empty of people in winter.

If I had time after classes, I'd often walk along the shoreline trail at sunset, watching the sky turn color behind the huge Douglas-firs and seeing the city lights blink on across English Bay. It was a good way to sort out my thoughts on essays that were due or write bad poetry about life in the city. After a few walks, I couldn't help but notice an impressive

natural event that happened along the beach every evening—
a gathering of crows.

As the sun sank low in the sky, small groups of crows
flew in from various directions to gather in a larger flock on
the beach and lawns. As each new group arrived, some from
the larger group would fly up to meet them, the birds greeting each other with excited caws and fancy flying antics such
as barrel rolls. It struck me immediately that these birds were
having a good time. This was crow happy hour after a long day
of collecting acorns, beachcombing for mussels, and serious
dumpster diving. As a budding biologist, I knew I shouldn't
attribute human thoughts of games and play to mere animals,
but playing is precisely what these birds were doing.

Several times I saw them playing a game in which one
would drop an empty mussel shell from a good height. Another
crow would swoop in and catch it before it hit the ground
then fly up and drop the shell for the next player to snatch it.
Another game was a crow version of King of the Castle, where
one crow would hang off the end of a weeping willow branch.
Another would fly in and knock it off its perch and hang in
its place until supplanted by the next in line. These sorts of
games went on for a half-hour or so until the cawing suddenly
increased in volume and the flock took off in a great black
horde, flying off to the south to some unknown roosting site
in the forests of Point Grey.

I enjoyed watching these nightly events and even wrote a
term paper for one of my biology classes on the timing of the
final flight to the roost. Not surprisingly, the flight took place a
certain time after sunset each night, the birds adjusting to the

changing day length with ease. On cloudy days they left earlier because of the lower light levels. I was proud of the tightness of the data and my minor discovery until an arts major friend pointed out that Shakespeare knew all about this phenomenon when he wrote *Macbeth*: "Light thickens, and the crow / Makes wing to the rooky wood."

Crows, along with their kin the jays, ravens, and magpies, are among the most intelligent of birds. Crows raised in human families can pick up words quite easily. A friend once dragged me out of my tent long before I wanted to leave the warmth of my sleeping bag, insisting that I help him identify a bird that had awoken him by saying "hello." I groggily complained that he was probably hearing a loon out on the lake, but sure enough, coming from a tree above his tent was something clearly wishing us "hello." After circling the tree I managed to get a good look at the speaker, and of course it was a crow. The following year I heard a crow calling "mama." Both these birds had likely been raised by people as pets then were released or escaped back into the wild.

There are many stories of the intelligence of crows. They commonly drop nuts and shells on road surfaces to crack them open, but I did hear a story that suggested they could go one better than that. When I was working in the Zoology Department at the University of British Columbia, a man called me to report that the crows in his neighborhood would pick up walnuts from the ground, then fly to a powerline that crossed a street. The birds would position themselves in front of an approaching car, then drop the nut in front of it, hoping the wheels would crush the hard shell.

There are three kinds of crows in North America. The American crow is the most widespread, found almost everywhere south of the Arctic. The northwestern crow lives along the Pacific coast from Alaska south to Washington; its Atlantic equivalent is the fish crow, found in the southeastern United States. The northwestern crow was likely founded by a small population of American crows that ventured across the Coast Mountains and Cascade Range and found the rich beaches and intertidal zone of the Pacific Northwest to their liking. Separated from their ancestors by miles of rain forest and snowy mountain peaks, they differentiated over the past few thousand years into a smaller, more gregarious species than the American crow.

In the past 150 years, however, those rain forests have been cleared along the Columbia and Fraser rivers and around Puget Sound. Coastal crows have met up again with their long-lost cousins and appear to interbreed freely. The situation is so confusing to birders in Washington that they have given up on trying to separate the two species. In British Columbia, contact between the two forms is much more restricted by the Fraser Canyon, and birdwatchers can still appreciate the smaller size and hoarser voice of the northwestern crow. Just where the boundary between the two lies is still very much open to debate, however. The range of the fish crow overlaps that of the American crow almost completely, yet the birds seem to keep themselves separate. Those two forms were likely physically separated for a much longer time before geographical and habitat barriers were removed, giving time for the factors that prevent interbreeding to develop.

Crows are one of the few kinds of native birds that have clearly benefited from the dramatic habitat changes affecting North America since the arrival of European settlers. Since they prefer open country over dense forests, logging and farming are both beneficial. Their omnivorous tastes also allow them to enjoy cornfields, landfills, and fast-food outlets. And their intelligence and adaptability have let them move into urban habitats totally different from any their ancestors would have experienced.

In the last thirty years this overall population growth has slowed, but there has been a dramatic movement of rural crows into the cities, paralleling the path of their human counterparts. There have certainly been changes to the crow flocks since I watched them in Vancouver in the 1970s. Where I used to consider a flock of five hundred crows to be a major gathering, I can now watch a line of more than ten thousand crows streaming into a roost in the Vancouver suburbs.

Another factor that put the brakes on crow population increases in North America has been the spread of West Nile Virus across the continent. This mosquito-borne illness originated in Uganda and has spread through Europe and western Asia in the last few decades. In 1999 a strain of the disease appeared in New York, likely brought from Israel. West Nile Virus produces little or no effect in most people, but about 1 percent of infected humans, primarily older people, develop a serious, polio-like illness.

It is primarily a disease of birds, and crows are one of the most susceptible species. Crows are not good carriers of West Nile Virus simply because they die too quickly to pass the disease on to another mosquito. Crow populations declined for three years after West Nile Virus reached North America, but the downward trend seems to have stabilized in the last two years, perhaps as more birds are becoming resistant to the disease.

Although some hard-hearted souls would be happy to hear that crow numbers are dropping, anyone who has made an effort to get to know these intelligent birds would be saddened by such news. I remember listening to a biologist speaking at a conference tearfully relate how her individually marked population of crows in Oklahoma was wiped out by West Nile Virus in late 2002 and 2003. She was not so much upset at the loss of her research but at the unexpected deaths of birds she knew personally. Because when you get to know crows individually, it's hard not to think of them as mental equals.

GOLDEN EAGLE

*O*NE OF THE real pleasures of birding is occasionally showing off your home turf to a visiting birder. That pleasure is even greater when you live in an area considered a birding mecca, and the Okanagan Valley is such a place. It has a breeding bird diversity as high as any location in North America, and several of its birds are found nowhere else in Canada.

I remember one such time, a sunny day in late March a few years ago. Steve Wilcox, a colleague of mine from Ontario, was on his first trip out West. It was very early spring, but there were enough early migrants and year-round residents to easily keep him happy. We started off in the south end of the valley, walking through fragrant sage, hoping in vain for an early sage thrasher. The light on the rock bluffs to the north was glorious, so we drove that direction and stopped above a small lake to look for chukar, a species of partridge adapted to these dry, stony hills. The lake held a small number of ducks and four magnificent tundra swans while a Say's phoebe gave its mournful call from the hillside. Finding no chukar, we drove a little farther on and stopped again near a low pass in the grasslands.

I quickly heard the low cackling of a male chukar, so we scanned the bluffs and found him standing on a small prominence, surveying his domain. I was setting up the scope for a better look when my colleague pointed out two young golden eagles soaring high above. Just as I picked them out, one of them tilted sideways and began plunging directly toward us. I lowered my binoculars to take in the whole scene and suddenly realized what it was after. The swans had left the lake behind us and were flying over the pass, on their way to Arctic breeding grounds. They saw the eagle's dive as well and immediately emptied their wings and fell toward us.

What had been a quiet pastoral scene moments before was now one of high drama. The swans pulled out of their dives just above the ground and were now flying through the sagebrush at waist height a few yards ahead of us, the pumping sound of their pinions clearly audible over the spring breeze. The eagle, perhaps seeing us at the last minute, veered off behind, the air through its primaries making a sound like tearing paper as it abandoned its high-speed stoop. Steve turned and smiled at me as if to say, "So this is what the West is all about," but I assured him that it wasn't always quite so spectacular. I was still shaking with excitement at the scene we had just witnessed.

I must admit I think golden eagles are the most impressive birds in my part of the world. Since I'm known as a bit of a bird nut, I'm often asked the question, "If you were a bird, which species would you like to be?" I always answer, "Golden

eagle." Who wouldn't want to spend his or her days soaring over some of the most beautiful scenery on the planet, climbing mountains with the twitch of a few primary feathers?

This fascination with golden eagles began early in my life. When I was perhaps twelve years old or so, a friend of my father's told him of an eagle nest above his orchard. My father was keen to get some photographs of the birds, and we drove out there the next weekend. Unlike many golden eagle nests, this one was reasonably accessible; we had to make a stiff climb up a very steep mountainside but were soon perched on the cliff top, only a few feet above the big stick nest. The cliff overhung somewhat, so you had to crawl to the edge and look down and back into the face to see the nest, something that my acrophobic knees did not appreciate. So I lay on the rock, enjoying the close views of the adults as they soared by. For the first time I saw the glowing golden hackles on the back of the birds' necks that gave them their name and heard the loud but amusingly songbird-like chirps they gave in agitation. I also remember the eagle's-eye view of the valley, watching the violet-green swallows flit below us, their emerald and purple backs shining in the sun.

Some people might be surprised at my choice of golden eagle over the bald eagle. The latter species certainly gets more press in North America, its image showing up everywhere from coats-of-arms to bumper stickers. But the golden is superior on several counts. Firstly, to my eyes it is a much more elegant bird, with a graceful leaflike shape to its wings. The wings are also held slightly above the horizontal, giving it a more interesting flight pattern. The bald eagle, by contrast, has a more utilitarian look to its rectangular, board-like wings held straight out from the body.

Secondly, if I had to be a bird, I'd much prefer the golden eagle's fare of fresh meat over the fruits of the bald eagle's scavenging habits—such delicacies as rotting fish and seal carcasses. Golden eagles generally kill their own meals, scanning the mountain slopes for rabbits or marmots, whereas bald eagles first check the beach to see what washed up overnight. I do see golden eagles lording over road-killed deer, but it is still fresh venison and not moldy salmon.

In September 1983 I climbed Sheep Mountain, a ridge beside Kluane Lake in the southwestern Yukon. It was a glorious sunny fall day, with a light breeze out of the northwest. We were looking for the namesake of the mountain—Dall sheep, the beautiful white thinhorn sheep of the far north, and were not disappointed. We reveled in the magnificent view of the cobalt-blue lake, set in the Shakwak Trench, a long, linear valley extending northwest to Alaska. I also remember watching a golden eagle sail by on the wind, sliding south, hardly moving a feather. I thought at the time it must be migrating south for the winter but had no idea then that it was part of one of the most spectacular bird movements in North America.

Almost a decade after my Yukon trip, Peter Sherrington and Des Allen were conducting a bird survey in March 1992 at Mount Lorette in the Rocky Mountains just west of Calgary. Their curiosity was piqued by a series of single golden eagles soaring across the valley in short succession. They decided to stay the whole day to watch the eagles and were astounded to count more than a hundred, all going the same direction on the same path. They returned two days later with more observers and counted 247 in a single afternoon. Peter and Des had stumbled upon a major eagle highway; before that, golden eagle migration in North America was considered a minor flight involving few birds. That fall, Peter organized a serious migration watch at Mount Lorette and tallied over two thousand eagles moving south along exactly the same route. A full survey the following spring counted 4,563 eagles, and subsequent counts in an adjacent valley suggest that more than six thousand eagles are involved in this mass flight.

These eagles are using predictable updrafts along the thrust-faulted ridges of the Canadian Rockies—massive blocks of rock that extend for hundreds of miles—to fly to and from wintering grounds in the southwestern United States. On their flight in spring they turn northwest at the north end of the Canadian Rockies and soar through the mountains of the southern Yukon to Kluane Lake, then up the Shakwak Trench to Alaska. There are very few sites elsewhere in the world with such a precise routing of migrant birds—the Bosporus, Gibraltar, and the isthmus of Panama are famous examples. At those sites continental geography forces the birds into certain paths around seas and oceans, but the eagles use the Rocky Mountain route simply because the topography makes flying so easy.

Excited by his survey group's initial findings, Peter organized the Rocky Mountain Eagle Research Foundation, which now coordinates migration censuses every year. Because golden eagles use the same route in spring and fall, the observers can accurately monitor both the numbers of eagles making the trip as well as the ratio of young and adult birds.

They can do the latter because golden eagles take four years to attain their dark brown plumage. Young birds have a very distinctive pattern of white spots at the base of the primary feathers in the wing and a white base to their tails. With those data, we can get an index of how good the breeding season has been each year. And because eagles are at the top of the food chain, the health of their populations provide an accurate report card of how the subarctic environment in a huge part of the continent is faring.

The route of migrating golden eagles in western North America has been confirmed by high technology—satellite radio transmitters attached to birds in Alaska. But the importance of this migratory route and the tremendous monitoring data it has generated would never have come to light without the initial curiosity of a couple of birders and the subsequent dedication and hard work of hundreds more. We need more birders!

WHITE-TAILED PTARMIGAN

*I*N LATE AUGUST 1978 I hiked with my brothers into one of the most beautiful landscapes on this earth, the southern Chilcotin Mountains. The peaks had beckoned us all summer as we worked on the pine-covered plateau to the north, their snowfields, meadows, and long ridges promising an alpine adventure second to none. We drove south and west into the Nemaiah Valley, unpacked our gear, and followed a faint trail up Elkin Creek to an unnamed but postcard-beautiful lake at treeline. The lake lay in a broad cirque valley carved out by an alpine glacier that had once flowed off the eastern flank of Mount Tatlow, the highest peak in the Chilcotin, one of the sculptural strokes that gave the mountain its beautiful pyramidal shape. The glacier had retreated over the past few centuries to small, sparkling patches of permanent ice and snow, and the valley was carpeted in green grass and late summer flowers.

We set up camp on the lakeshore and decided to try catching some supper. A few tosses of a fishing line (literally tosses—we had no rod) produced a panful of cutthroat trout, so we were soon enjoying fresh fish and rice with a side dish of the finest scenery you could imagine. We scanned the mountain and decided that next day we would make the long climb to the peak, not knowing at the time that Tatlow was considered sacred by the Chilcotin people and it was bad luck to even look straight at the mountain, let alone climb it.

Next morning we awoke to a totally different world. Gone were the blue lake, green meadows, and azure sky, replaced by a fresh fall of snow and thick fog. We decided to hike around the lake instead of climbing the mountain, knowing that we couldn't get lost that way. We hadn't gone far before my brother Syd called out "Ptarmigan!" Rob and I hurried over, and there were a half-dozen small, gray-brown grouse huddled among the snow-covered rocks. When hiking in the mountains I consider myself lucky to find more than one or two ptarmigan in a day, but that morning we counted over sixty in our circumnavigation of the little lake.

These were white-tailed ptarmigan, the species found in alpine habitats in the mountains of western North America. Two other species, willow ptarmigan and rock ptarmigan, are found in similar Arctic and subarctic habitats around the Northern Hemisphere. Normally ptarmigan are almost impossible to see, blending in perfectly with the lichen-covered stones; in autumn they molt into a pure-white winter plumage that lets them nestle unseen against the snow. Because of their ability to melt into the background and the relative inaccessibility of their mountain homes, white-tailed ptarmigan rank very high on the "most wanted" lists of birders, and some of my friends have spent years searching before finally finding one. So it was definitely a treat to see so many in one day, but I couldn't attribute our success to keen eyesight—these birds had been caught out by the early snowfall, and their dark shapes contrasted sharply with the white meadows.

I've looked for ptarmigan many times, and on most occasions I've had to be satisfied with a feather or two or a pile of toothpaste-like droppings. Ironically, my first sighting of a ptarmigan was an event that I almost didn't want to happen. The only easily accessible peak with ptarmigan in my boyhood neighborhood was Apex Mountain, a high ridge that barely rose above treeline. My father had found ptarmigan there, but every time we went there as a family the little grouse failed to show. Then one summer my brother Syd and I spent a few days showing a visiting birder around the Okanagan Valley. He had a list of species that he wanted to see and one by one we found them for him. By the last day he had only one species left on the list—white-tailed ptarmigan.

I told him that we could look for ptarmigan on Apex but warned him that our chances were slim. By then my enthusiasm for finding birds for him had declined considerably, cooled off by his seeming complete disinterest in birds that were not on his want list. So, even though ptarmigan would be a life bird for me, I secretly hoped we wouldn't find one that day. We hiked all over the mountain meadows, watching horned larks feed their young and finding a mountain bluebird nest in the forestry lookout at the top. Late in the afternoon, not surprisingly, we had still not found a ptarmigan, and feeling somewhat relieved, we called it a day and headed back to the car. Just as we reached it a ptarmigan sauntered out of the heather and strolled across the track in front of us. The birder casually checked it off his list, and we headed home. Syd and I rolled our eyes at his luck and apparent lack of appreciation for the moment.

Although alpine ridges make glorious hiking routes, living off the land there can be a harsh existence. There are few other birds and mammals that share this habitat with ptarmigan, and all the other birds leave in late summer for winter holidays in warmer climates. A raven might occasionally fly over, on its way to another watershed, or a couple of nutcrackers may be squawking downslope, looking for seed caches. Most of the mammals are beneath the snow or have moved to lower elevations. In fact, if you walk across an alpine ridge in western North America in winter, the only vertebrate you are likely to see is a ptarmigan.

Ptarmigan survive on willow buds all winter, their diet expanding to berries, leaves, and insects in summer. The young birds eat mainly insects and spiders as they quickly grow in July and August but switch to the adult diet as soon as they reach full size.

The small, round form of ptarmigan makes it easier for them to retain body heat in winter. Their feet are covered in a thick coat of feathers, not only to keep them warm but also to act as snowshoes. And their white winter plumage isn't just an adaptation to make them hard to see. Because they lack all pigments, the feathers are essentially hollow and are significantly better insulators than colored feathers. On top of that, ptarmigan spend a lot of time under the snow in winter. In fact, there are only two basic requirements for a good winter territory for ptarmigan: a ready supply of willow buds and reliable areas of deep snow for roosting.

Females tend to move downslope more than males each winter. Subalpine creek valleys have both snow and willows in abundance, so it's not surprising females move down into them. The males presumably stay higher to remain closer to territories that are important to maintain at all costs if they want to breed in the spring. I have only once seen a ptarmigan in its winter plumage, when only its black eyes and beak stand out against the snow. That bird, I surmise a female, was in hemlock rain forest at mid-elevations on the slopes of Mount Shuksan in the North Cascades. Needless to say, I was surprised to see it there amid the giant trees, although it did have a more than ample supply of deep snow.

Back on Mount Tatlow, the mid-morning sun had burned off the fog and the snow melted quickly. Our thoughts turned from ptarmigan to the mountain again, and we began our climb. I picked mountain sorrel leaves poking through the melting snow, their biting sourness sending a burst of saliva into my dry mouth. We left the ptarmigan behind on the sloping ridges and entered steeper boulder fields above the range of the prostrate willows.

By noon we had reached the tiny, pyramidal summit. The peak cornice didn't seem that stable—Syd broke off a section that exposed a view to the rocks and ice far below—so we descended a short way to have more room to relax with our lunches. Before us spread the Chilcotin Plateau, an ocean of lodgepole pine on a flat plain of basalt, the crystalline result of a series of vast lava flows that flooded the plateau over the last twenty million years. To the south was a more tumultuous sea of rock and ice, the heart of the Coast Mountains.

Ignorant of the curse of Mount Tatlow, or Ts'il?os as is it known to the Chilcotin people, we descended with contented hearts. Looking back on that day, I can say that the only bad luck we encountered was the snowfall that delayed our ascent, and even that provided the opportunity to see more ptarmigan than I'm likely to ever see again. I haven't returned to Ts'il?os but have admired it from a distance, happy that the mountain and all its ptarmigan are now preserved in a stunning provincial park.

HORNED LARK

*M*Y MOTHER'S FAMILY came from New-foundland. The Munns had been successful merchants in the town of Harbour Grace but lost most of their considerable wealth in the great Newfoundland banking disaster of 1894. After a decade or more of picking up the financial pieces, my grandparents decided to leave the island, drawn to a new life in British Columbia by idyllic promises of peach orchards and warm, sandy beaches. Although my mother was born shortly after their arrival in the Okanagan Valley, she never forgot her Atlantic heritage and constantly reminded her children of it. She even cooked up fish and brewis, that great Newfoundland comfort food, whenever she could get the essential ingredients delivered to British Columbia.

I was never that fond of fish and brewis—a hearty combination of salt cod and soaked hardtack drizzled with scrunchions and lassie (deep-fried pork back fat and molasses)—until I moved to Newfoundland to do postgraduate research. When I arrived in St. John's, I felt an immediate connection to the landscape. I loved the late-summer fog and the massive green waves of autumn storms coming into Middle Cove, and I felt a special affinity to the headland barrens along the coast. Chilled year-round by the cold waters of the Labrador Current, the growing season on these coastal hills is too short to support the germination of trees, and the shrieking winds of winter prune back the few seedlings that somehow get started. Those bleak stretches of tundra tugged at my soul, perhaps because they reminded me of my childhood in sagebrush grasslands.

My initial plan for graduate research in Newfoundland was to study the breeding ecology of black guillemots, small seabirds that nested along the rocky coast of the island. But when my thesis supervisor suggested that I continue some research a colleague had started on the breeding biology of horned larks, I jumped at the idea. These birds are the quintessential tundra songbird and in North America are found almost anywhere trees are not. I spent the next two years wandering across mossy barrens, becoming acquainted with Arctic plants and listening against the constant wind for the tinkling song of larks.

Larks do not like trees. There are ninety-two species around the world—each type of treeless habitat in Africa and Eurasia seems to have its own lark species, from the dune larks of coastal Namibia to the sky larks of the English countryside. The horned lark is found in tundra habitats across northern Eurasia and is the only lark to have colonized North America. It probably arrived from both east and west, immigrating to the Atlantic coast via Iceland and Greenland and to the western mountains through the tundra of Alaska. Once established on the continent, the horned lark found the prairies, deserts,

and dunes empty of larks and quickly filled those habitats with its own kind. There are now more than twenty recognized subspecies of horned lark in North America, each adapted to its own barren ecosystem.

I arrived on my Newfoundland study site on a sunny day in early April. Although sunny, it was not particularly warm, and the almost incessant wind was slamming against the sea cliffs. The last snowdrifts of winter were melting in the gullies and the first flowers opening to the sun. I began to explore the surroundings that would become so familiar to me over the next few months. The drier ridges were covered in moss and other cushion plants; the swales were filled with golden grass, ferns, and clumps of irises. Many of the plants looked familiar to me from my times in the alpine tundra of western Canada, but others were totally new. As I walked away from the sea, I began to see mats of twisted fir and spruce huddled in hollows where they would be protected from the wind. Newfoundlanders have their own word for this growth form—tuckamore—that is so common on their island. In the Rockies I had learned to call it krummholz, a German word meaning twisted wood.

I saw very few larks on my first day on the study site, and those that were present were busy feeding, perhaps hungry after their migratory journey from the eastern coast of the United States. By mid-April, though, the tundra was sprinkled with small flocks, and I began to hear the tinkling song of territorial male larks. It took longer to actually see them— they were singing so high in the sky they were merely specks against the deep blue. A male would sing for several minutes, circling high over the land he was claiming, then descend in one or two breathtakingly steep dives, swooping to land on a prominent rock. There he would continue singing in shorter bursts. The song-post rocks were spattered with bright orange lichen, a species that can only live where there is a regular supply of nitrogen, in this case from bird droppings. These rocks had been used by larks for millennia. The females were much more inconspicuous, walking between clumps of grass, feeding on last summer's pink crowberries and lingonberries (the latter known as partridge berry in Newfoundland). Their backs blended in perfectly with the dried grass, and I often didn't see them at all until they flew up in front of me, giving their clear flight calls.

Male and female horned larks look almost identical, but you can tell them apart in spring when the male's plumage is brighter and less streaked with brown. Both have a black mask and black necklace set off against a yellow background. They are pinkish brown above and have a jet-black tail with white edges. Like many ground-dwelling songbirds, their hind claws are surprisingly long, presumably giving them extra stability while walking.

My first task in my research was to find lark nests. I assumed that I would simply stumble on them by flushing incubating females up in front of me as I walked. But after a few days of fruitless efforts I realized that I would have to be more methodical about the task. When I saw a female foraging on the tundra I would sit down and simply watch her. Sometimes I would watch for an hour in vain before deciding that this was a female that simply didn't have a nest. But other females would act a little more anxious, pretending to feed for a minute or two, then flying off a short distance, feeding again, flying, then walking through the grass and disappearing. I would then slowly walk toward the spot I last saw them and carefully note the exact place they flew up from. I would spend several minutes combing the ground at that site, and if I was lucky I would find the nest—a small cup of grasses lined with feathers and wool, tucked into the lee of a grass clump. One striking feature of many nests was a small patio of flat pebbles on one side of the nest, likely placed there to camouflage the bare dirt dug out of the nest cup. In the nests were two to four small whitish eggs flecked with olive-brown.

From my long periods of watching female larks I soon learned that they have a characteristic flight when leaving the nest. Instead of climbing quickly and calling as they did when I approached them too closely while they were feeding, incubating birds would silently leave the nest when I was 50 meters or more from them, flying low over the ground so as not to attract attention. That knowledge saved me a lot of time, since I only had to sit and watch birds that were obviously nesting.

To study the larks' breeding behavior, I wanted to be able to identify individual birds. The standard method for doing that is to place small plastic bands on the birds' legs in different color combinations. Each bird would get the standard aluminum band with a unique number as well as three colored bands. For instance, one bird would have two blue bands on the left leg and a green band over the metal band on the right. This system is great, but it requires that one catch the birds.

I spent a lot of time trying to catch larks. My first strategy was to use mist-nets, fine nylon nets that are essentially invisible to flying birds when set up properly. I knew it would be a challenge to use mist-nets on the tundra; even on calm, cloudy days they are quite visible in open habitats where the black netting stands out against the gray sky. But the big problem was the wind, which billowed the net so that even a blind lark would know it was there, and if it actually hit the net it would probably just bounce out of the taut material. The wind rarely stopped; I even lost one furled net that collapsed in a gale and became hopelessly entangled in the vegetation.

I caught one or two males in improvised traps set on song-post rocks, but most wouldn't go near the contraptions. The only method that worked was catching the females on their nests at night. I would venture out into the dark (and very often foggy) night, armed with a flashlight and a butterfly net. Following stone cairns I would somehow manage to find the nest and carefully place the net over it. I soon had bands on all the females in the population and could at least follow their foraging travels throughout their territories. I had to content myself with following certain males through the day as they battled with neighboring birds, slowly building up a detailed map of the lark territories in the area. I found that birds often infringed on their neighbors' territories, perhaps not surprising in a habitat enveloped in thick fog for almost half of the daylight hours.

By early June most of the larks had nests underway and some were feeding young by the second week of June. Then disaster struck. On June 12 the ever-present wind rose to a howling 130 kilometers per hour. I huddled in my small house, listening to sleet and rain pummeling the windows. The next morning my stove was out of oil, but the wind was still shrieking. I ventured outside, bracing myself against the railings as

I filled my oil canister under the steps. All the while I kept thinking of the larks.

The wind died down to acceptable levels by nightfall, so I went out the following morning to check the nests. The three nests with young had been deserted, and the nestlings were dead. Four of the eight nests with eggs had been abandoned as well, but females were still incubating the other four. I suspect that the nests with incubating females had been abandoned to the elements during the gale, but the females had returned to them when the wind and rain abated. Female larks probably know instinctively that if eggs are incubated for a few days and begin to develop, they must be kept warm until they hatch or they will die. However, if incubation has barely begun, eggs can be left cold for several days and will begin development again when incubation resumes.

The birds that had lost nests to the storm immediately built new ones and laid replacement clutches. Within a week all seemed back to normal on the barrens. Larks, like other ground-nesting birds, try to get their young out of the nests as quickly as possible. This practice reduces the chance that the nest will be discovered by a weasel or a fox. The incubation period, the length of time it takes the lark eggs to hatch, is only slightly shorter than that for other birds—about eleven days compared with thirteen for a tree-nesting bird like a robin. But the nestling period is remarkably short—young larks grow very rapidly and within nine days are hopping away from the nest. They can't fly very well at that time, but their legs are fully developed and well muscled. Larks can have young out of the nest within twenty days of the beginning of incubation, almost a full week faster than most tree-nesting songbirds.

By the first of July most nests had fledged, the young following their parents as best they could, giving loud *breet* calls to let the adults know where they were and that they were hungry. About a quarter of the pairs laid second clutches of eggs once their first brood had fledged, but the rest contented themselves with keeping their brood well fed. Perhaps the number of second broods would have been higher if the storm hadn't set things back. Horned larks in more temperate climates regularly try to raise two or more broods per year, whereas those in the high Arctic raise only one brood but lay five eggs instead of two to four.

I followed the larks until September when I returned to the university campus in St. John's. I made two trips out to the barrens in the fall but both coincided with extraordinary storms that Newfoundland is famous for. On the first occasion I didn't reach the study area but found out the next week that winds there had been over 160 kilometers per hour that day. The wind was only blowing 120 kilometers per hour the day I did make it, and I saw only a few larks huddled in the grass. I quickly retreated back to the city, leaving the coastal tundra to the wind and sleet.

My love of the barrens was not diminished, but in the comfort of St. John's I also developed an enduring love for Newfoundland music and culture. I even grew to love fish and brewis and still make it whenever I can get the ingredients delivered to the British Columbia interior. Unfortunately the hardest ingredient to find now is not the bag of Purity hard bread, but the cod.

NORTHERN GANNET

*N*EWFOUNDLAND BARS often fill with the strains of "Let Me Fish Off Cape St. Mary's," both an anthem of Newfoundlanders' love of their land and sea and now a lament for a way of life that is gone forever. The lyrics speak of men in their dories on the broad swells of the North Atlantic, fishing with their friends and the ever-present seabirds. I lived for one glorious year in the lighthouse at Cape St. Mary's and spent many hours lying in the grass at the edge of the high cliffs, huddled below the constant gale, gazing out to sea. To the south were the dark blue waters of the Grand Banks, to the west the distant shorelines of the Burin Peninsula and the French island of Saint Pierre, and to the east a spire of rock covered in white birds—six thousand northern gannets.

On my first trip to Cape St. Mary's I drove the rough gravel road down the Cape Shore with a colleague, stopping at every cape and viewpoint to census seabirds. In the 1970s the road was quite rough, each outport a cluster of colorful houses tucked into a sheltered cove. I was new to Newfoundland then and had a hard time understanding the local dialects. Residents of the Cape Shore spoke with a strong Irish accent with its own local eccentricities, including saying *gewse* and *mewse* instead of *goose* and *moose*. The lightkeeper at the Cape was from the other side of Placentia Bay and spoke Burin, an old English dialect. One phrase I remember was "Don't 'inder I!", used in place of the universal "Interference" in games. The lightkeeper claimed not to understand his assistant from the Cape Shore and would occasionally ask me—I assume in jest—to translate.

The Cape Shore men were all fishermen in those days, going out in their longliners to catch cod. On most days there was quite a flotilla off the Cape. Early in the morning several boats would come in close to the cliffs to shoot eiders and murres (called turrs in Newfoundland), even though it was officially a bird sanctuary. The lightkeeper complained about this practice, but one foggy day I saw him dispatching disoriented murres with a two-by-four, and he invited me to come on over later for some turr pie.

It was a long walk to the gannet stack, the trail winding through grassy headland tundra dotted with sheep. The cliffs below the trail were lined with countless kittiwakes, their elegant nests clinging to impossibly narrow ledges. With the kittiwakes were the murres, standing like little penguins on the ledges. The murres built no nests at all, each pair guarding a single egg on the bare rock—a pointy egg designed to roll in a tight circle when nudged. When it wasn't windy at the Cape it was foggy, and the only indication that you were close to tens of thousands of seabirds was the constant, throbbing din and the sharp smell of guano. Occasionally the wail of the kittiwakes would rise to a loud mournful chord when a raven slipped in to steal an egg for breakfast. The growling cacophony of the gannets increased to a magnificent crescendo as the trail turned onto a small rampart of rock that jutted toward the stack, and suddenly the spectacle was right in front of you: big white birds sailing through the air, thousands jostling on the rock a short distance away.

Like the men in dories and longliners off the Cape, gannets are expert fishers. They are goose-sized but have a graceful shape and powerful flight that belie their large size. Gannets are one of the handsomest of birds, with a dense, snow-white plumage offset by jet-black wingtips, a saffron-tinted head, and silver-blue eyes. They are streamlined in all four quarters—a long pointed bill, pointed wings, and pointed tail. This shape is essential for their amazing fishing technique. They fly high over the ocean, constantly looking down into the dark waters for schooling fish and squid. When they see the flash of a silver school, they turn into the wind, dip one wing, and are suddenly plunging vertically toward the sea. Tucking both wings in close to their body, they drop like white missiles. At the last second, they throw both wings back so that the tips extend beyond the long tail and hit the surface with a surprisingly small splash—they would receive high marks at an Olympic diving competition.

The speed of entry carries them 3 meters or so underwater; if that isn't enough to catch the fish they can swim deeper in pursuit of their prey. Snatching the fish, they swallow it underwater. If they are unsuccessful, they launch themselves into the air and try again. The actions of a few diving gannets attract more and more so that soon there are fifty or a hundred frantically plunging into the cold water in a feeding frenzy.

The well-fed gannet returns to the colony, flying with others in long lines low over the water. At the colony, the bird must pick its landing spot precisely, for the stack is wall-to-wall gannets, and neighbors can be highly incensed if a bird lands in the wrong place. Once it lands beside its mate an elaborate greeting ritual ensues, the birds facing each other and clacking their bills together in a behavior known as mutual fencing.

The nests are all one peck-length apart, and neighbors are continually jabbing at each other to maintain that distance. Occasionally a more serious fight will break out, especially if a new male tries to take over an established nest site. I witnessed one bloody battle in which an intruding bird was grabbed by several birds on all sides and couldn't get away. I eventually left before the tussle ended, but it looked like it was going to end badly for the intruder. Sometimes these intrusions are necessary as the birds take off from the plateau at the top of the colony—they have to take a few running steps, incurring the wrath of brooding birds as they trot by.

The female lays a single egg in the nest, and the male and female take turns incubating it, wrapping their black, webbed feet around the egg. Their feet have an increased blood supply at this time, much as other birds form a brood patch on their bellies. This interesting way to incubate eggs is unique to the gannets and their immediate relatives, the boobies, pelicans, and cormorants. The hatchlings are small and helpless but put on weight quickly and at ten weeks of age weigh 50 percent more than the adults. That baby fat is gradually turned into feathers and lean flight muscle; the young birds leave the nest in a one-way flight to sea in late September or October when they are about three months old. That first flight is a bit erratic, and the birds hit the ocean with an inelegant splash; from that moment on they are independent of their parents and simply swim off into the Atlantic on their own.

In an era when all the news coming out of the sea seems to be very negative, the trend in gannet numbers is refreshingly positive. The northwest Atlantic population, which breeds in six colonies off the coast of Quebec and Newfoundland, has increased by 50 percent over the last twenty years. When I lived at Cape St. Mary's in the mid-1970s the breeding colony was restricted to Bird Rock, but I was heartened to see a significant expansion onto adjacent cliffs when I last visited in 1999.

This increase is mostly a rebound from artificially low populations caused by persecution in the early 1900s as well as the effects of pesticides. Although gannets were never used for food as many seabirds on the Atlantic coast were, they were routinely killed by fishermen at sea and at the colonies. If the bodies were retrieved at all they were simply cut up for fish bait. Organochlorine pesticides such as DDT had a significant impact on gannet breeding success in the 1960s. These chemicals accumulate in animals at the top of the food chain such as the gannet and in birds cause a thinning of eggshells, resulting in breakage and a low hatching success. Since DDT was banned in North America in the 1970s, organochlorine levels have declined dramatically in gannets and hatching success has doubled.

As I lay in the cliff-top grass at Cape St. Mary's, watching the gannets fly out to sea in the teeth of a June gale, I couldn't help but think—these are birds in their element. I was definitely out of my element, surviving only because my oil stove was a few feet behind me in a cozy house. These birds were skimming the colossal waves on their long, white wings, tacking against the howling winds, going fishing as gannets had been doing for tens of thousands of years.

But Newfoundland and the seas that surround it are changing rapidly. Humans have effectively removed many species from the Atlantic—first the whales, then the salmon, then the cod. Although small numbers of these species remain, they cannot play their former pivotal roles in shaping the North Atlantic ecosystem. And there are new concerns that global warming may further alter ocean currents in dramatic and unpredictable ways, changing the ecosystem forever.

The human communities have already changed completely. The moratorium on cod fishing has driven many of the fishermen from the Cape Shore and other parts of the Newfoundland coast to work in other industries across Canada. Federal funds designed to soften this blow have been used to cover the brightly painted outport houses in pastel vinyl siding. The lightkeepers are gone at the Cape, replaced by a large interpretive center for the seabird colony, and the rough Cape Shore road is now a paved highway. Even the dialects are slowly disappearing as children grow up watching cable television or follow their families out of the outports. For now the gannets still flourish, perhaps eating small fish formerly consumed by cod. But will there be gannets at Cape St. Mary's a thousand years from now?

TUFTED PUFFIN

On the Pacific coast of Canada, about 50 kilometers off the northern tip of Vancouver Island, lies one of the most remarkable islands in the country. Triangle Island is only 1 kilometer wide, rising steeply from the cold ocean waters to a point about 200 meters above sea level. Its green but treeless slopes are cloaked in a wind-carved blanket of salmonberry, salal, and hairgrass.

With no safe anchorage and almost no flat land above the high-tide line, Triangle Island is rarely visited by humans. At the highest point on the island is the concrete base of a former lighthouse tower, built in 1910 and dismantled in 1920 after a decade of fruitless battles against the elements. Life on the island was almost impossible for the lightkeepers; the horrific winds blew almost everything away, and supply ships were often months late, leading to near-starvation. And the light itself was essentially useless—it was so high above the sea that during bad weather it was always hidden in clouds and fog.

But like the gannets at Cape St. Mary's, seabirds revel in the wind and weather off the British Columbia coast, and every spring over a million of them return to Triangle Island to nest. But the scene is entirely different than the bird-covered cliffs of Newfoundland—on Triangle the nests are mostly hidden beneath the grass and almost all the action happens at night. The entire island is honeycombed with burrows dug by Cassin's auklets, tiny seabirds little bigger than starlings that feed on shrimp-like animals called euphausiids. With over 500,000 auklet burrows in the island turf, you have to be careful where you put your feet so that you don't break through the surface, destroying the nest and possibly your ankle as well.

The Cassin's auklets feed by day. As night approaches they gather in large flocks offshore then fly into their nests after dark. They are not particularly agile fliers—auks are adapted more for flying underwater than in the air—and they more or less crash-land into the grass and salmonberry on the steep slopes, then scramble to their burrows.

Two other members of the auk family nest in more localized parts of the island. The steep grassy slopes above the south beach are home to about forty thousand pairs of rhinoceros auklets, and about thirty thousand pairs of tufted puffins burrow in the turf of Puffin Rock, a rugged islet that is attached to the southwest corner of Triangle Island at low tide. The rhinoceros auklet, or rhino as it is simply called by seabird biologists, is really a nocturnal puffin, a heavy-set, blackish bird with a yellow bill that carries a conspicuous horn in the breeding season. Like the Cassin's auklets, they return to their burrows at night, but unlike the small auklets, their size makes them rather dangerous projectiles as they rocket into the island like a cloud of small, heavy footballs. Biologists tend to avoid the south slope at night if they can.

Although they are only the third most populous bird on the island, tufted puffins are the poster children of Triangle because of their outlandish bills and plumage and because they are active during the day around their burrows. It was puffins—or rather, a visit with my friend Anne Vallée, who was studying them—that drew me to Triangle Island in 1981.

I flew out to the island on a sunny day in early August. The helicopter left Port Hardy and motored over Cape Scott, the northern tip of Vancouver Island, then over the larger, forested islands of the Scott group—Lanz and Cox. We flew high; the pilot explained that if the engine quit he'd rather be able to autorotate to dry land than ditch into the rough seas. We could see the pyramidal shape of Triangle Island ahead as we passed over Beresford and Sartine Islands, essentially grass-covered rocks ringed by basking sea lions. Although it was noon and most of the birds were at sea, Triangle Island was an air-traffic-control nightmare—birds buzzing by in all directions, most of them at high speed. We descended very slowly to allow the birds to see us—we didn't want a puffin through the windshield or an eagle in the tail rotor.

I was on the island for one glorious week and hiked all over it with Anne and her assistant Robin Cohen. We climbed to the base of the old light tower, down to the precipitous north shores, then across the neck of land to Puffin Rock. It was quite a scramble to the top of the Rock, but there were gently sloping grassy slopes at the top, dotted with nesting gulls and tufted puffins. Tucked into the rock cliffs were a couple of horned puffins, a more northern species that is very rare in Canadian waters. Anne showed me the common murre colony on the northwest cliffs—this was a bit of the island like Cape St. Mary's, with birds shoulder to shoulder along rock ledges. She casually pointed out a few thick-billed murres nesting among the common murres—I was ecstatic to see these birds here. Like the horned puffins, they are more northern birds and although they are abundant in Arctic waters, they had never been found nesting on Canada's Pacific coast before.

But I was always drawn back to the tufted puffins. I had never been so close to puffins before and was enthralled by their enormous orange bills and blond plumes. The birds were flying in with mouthfuls of food for the young, sailing on stubby wings into the ever-present wind. Single birds and small groups sat on the edge of the steep hillside among the thigh-high tufts of grass. When we approached one sitting next to the cliff, it launched itself into the air with whirring wings and plummeted downward as if in an elevator with a broken cable. As it began its fall, it gave a low *arrrr* call as if its stomach were uncomfortable with the sudden drop, but in a second it had reached flight speed and arced away from the island.

Anne reached into several puffin burrows—they are usually about a meter long—and retrieved the single nestling in each to measure its growth. Most were close to fledging size.

One puffin I managed to get close to was clearly carrying large shrimp-like animals in its beak—probably euphausiids. The adult puffins feed predominantly on euphausiids around Triangle Island but tend to feed their young more small fish such as sand lance. They feed some distance from the colony— sometimes 50 kilometers or more—wherever they can find concentrations of suitable prey. Like all members of the auk family, puffins can dive deeply to catch their fish, and although they have webbed feet, they use their wings to propel themselves down, literally flying underwater. Tufted puffins get down to 60 meters below the surface on most dives and can probably go to twice that depth if they have to.

Because they have such a distance to fly for food, the adults like to carry a full load back to their single chick. A normal load is about five or six fish, but they can carry more than twenty small fish at times. After catching one fish, a puffin will hold it in place with its rough tongue while pursuing the second. Each parent usually makes two trips to the nest each day, so the nestlings get four meals daily. The young grow steadily in good years and quickly turn from blackish puffballs to dusky versions of the adults. When the adults feel their youngster is ready to leave the burrow, they simply stop feeding it. Over a day or two it lives off its considerable fat stores, continuing to lengthen its flight feathers and develop its flight muscles. The young birds come to the burrow entrance and exercise their wings while they wait for the absent parents. Finally, drawn by hunger or some deeper instinct, the juvenile bird walks to the cliff edge, launches into the air, and flutters down into the blue Pacific. It must learn to catch fish and survive the elements on its own.

After breeding, all the puffins migrate into the center of the North Pacific Ocean, where they spend the winter eating squid, small fish, and euphausiids. Since their Canadian breeding colonies are so remote, tufted puffins are rarely seen by casual observers. But studies have shown that their breeding success and population numbers might be an important indicator of the health of our oceans. Like Goldilocks and the three bears' porridge, puffins prefer oceans that are not too cold and not too hot. Nestling growth and survival rates are especially poor when the surface sea temperatures are too warm, as they were from 1995 to 1998.

There are many indications that the oceans of the world are steadily warming, and incursions of warm water north along the Pacific coast of North America are becoming more and more the norm. Birders notice this phenomenon all the time—the number of brown pelicans reported on the British Columbia coast is rising every decade, and an adult magnificent frigatebird, the archetypal bird of the tropical oceans, was recently seen soaring over southern Vancouver Island. The puffin population on Triangle Island seems to be stable for the moment, but declines may be masked by the fact that puffins are long-lived birds, and several decades may pass before the effects of persistent breeding failure are noticed. Puffin numbers have declined drastically in recent years in California, Oregon, and Washington and logic would suggest that British Columbia populations may soon show significant decreases.

It is difficult and often dangerous work to monitor the health of the oceans. Anne Vallée fell to her death from a cliff on the north side of Triangle Island the summer after I visited her; the island is now also called the Anne Vallée Ecological Reserve. The oceans are the source of almost all our weather and much of our food, and we must continue the work of Anne and others to understand the complex processes that keep them in balance. And an islandful of well-fed young tufted puffins may be one of the best indicators that things are going in the right direction off the coast of British Columbia.

BLACK-FOOTED ALBATROSS

*I*N AUGUST 1987 I made an ill-fated attempt to return to Triangle Island. I wanted to show a group of ten keen birders the avian spectacle I had seen six years previously. This time we took a high-speed dive boat from Port Hardy. The captain said that we would be at the island in time for lunch and back in Port Hardy before dark. We raced northwest up Goletas Channel at 20 knots on flat waters protected by Nigei and Hope islands. There was little wind, and hopes were high that the crossing to Triangle would be relatively smooth. A Leach's storm-petrel fluttered by, a dark swallow-like seabird rarely encountered by day in coastal waters, adding to the anticipation of the crowd. But when we crossed Nahwitti Bar, where Goletas Channel ends and the open Pacific begins, we encountered high swells from a recent storm. Our speed dropped to 9 or 10 knots, and most of us began to look as blue-green as the water.

As we made slow progress against the swells, I began to realize that we weren't going to get to Triangle that day. The birding was good, though, and we kept our spirits up by pointing out seabirds that are not often seen from land in

British Columbia—first a fork-tailed storm-petrel dancing over the water, then thirty northern fulmars and three hundred sooty shearwaters sailing by on stiffly held wings. We started to see birds that were probably on foraging trips from Triangle Island—ten tufted puffins, fifteen Cassin's auklets, two hundred common murres, and five hundred rhinoceros auklets scattered on the water, diving for fish and euphausiids. Four pomarine jaegers and a red phalarope flew by, on their way from high Arctic breeding grounds to winter quarters in the tropical Pacific.

The captain took me aside and suggested that we anchor in the lee of Cox Island to have lunch, then return to Port Hardy. I heartily agreed, since I knew Triangle was out of the question because of our slow speed in the waves, and the prospect of a protected anchorage gave my stomach hope for the future. Moments later the engine suddenly stopped. The captain and his mate removed the engine cowling, filling the deck with thick diesel fumes. The boat bobbed and pitched in the high swells, and the landlubber birders, myself included, headed for the rails. Thoughts of lunch vanished along with our breakfasts. Green waves came over the stern, soaking us to the waist, and we didn't care. We slowly drifted toward the rocky coast of Cape Scott while the captain radioed the Coast Guard.

In the midst of the agony of mal de mer, I clearly remember one image—a huge dark seabird sailing out of the west to investigate our boat. Someone shouted "Black-footed albatross!", and ten pallid faces turned to the bird. It dwarfed the shearwaters with its 2.1-meter wingspan and hardly moved a feather as it banked over the waves. Quickly sensing that we were not a fishboat and had no decent food to offer, the albatross turned back to the western horizon. The birders on board forgot their troubles for a moment—some had never seen an albatross before and none saw them often. The captain perked up too as he discovered the cause of our engine problems—a loose belt in the water pump pulley. We turned and limped home with a rescue boat escorting us and the mate wearing out a good pair of shoes to keep tension on the spinning belt.

By evening we were back in Port Hardy. We laughed over dinner about our misadventures, deeply disappointed that Triangle Island had eluded us but excited to have seen birds of the open ocean. The albatross had saved the day.

Black-footed albatrosses fly the North Pacific Ocean. Albatrosses are designed for life on the open seas and use the one reliable source of energy available on the surface of subtropical and temperate waters—the wind—to carry them great distances in search of food. Albatrosses, like human-built gliders, have what aircraft engineers call high-aspect-ratio wings—in other words, long and thin. One of the biggest sources of drag on a wing comes from air spilling over the wingtip; long, thin wings minimize this effect by making the wingtip area small compared to the area of the entire wing. Albatrosses can therefore glide with wings locked for tremendous distances, using the lift from the winds over the waves to stay aloft. They are among the most fuel-efficient of world travelers; although the claim that they sleep on the wing is disputed, their energy expenditure aloft is very close to that while resting.

Most albatrosses are found in southern oceans, perhaps simply because there is more water and less land on that half of the globe. They are especially abundant in the cold subantarctic waters that are so rich in nutrients and thus albatross food. Conversely, they tend to avoid equatorial oceans because their warm waters are relatively empty of suitable prey and lack regular winds. Coleridge's ancient mariner found himself becalmed in these same doldrums, and perhaps the albatross he shot with his crossbow was a lost, doomed bird even before it encountered that ill-starred ship.

Black-footed albatrosses are found off the British Columbia coast in all months of the year, but are commonest in late summer and fall. In late October the breeding adults gather on the nesting colonies, most of them (sixty thousand pairs) on small islands in the Hawaiian island chain. There they begin a breeding cycle that lasts until the following July. Each female lays a single egg that takes more than nine weeks to hatch. Both adults take turns incubating the egg and brooding the young. When the nestling is small, one adult broods or guards the young while the other forages close to the colony, but once it is about eighteen days old the parents stop guarding it and begin to forage farther and farther away. Eventually they are each spending two weeks away from the chick in turns, so the chick is only fed once every week or so. Each feeding at this stage is very significant, the adult bringing up to 600 grams of food at a time.

Albatrosses take prey near the surface of the ocean, either upending like a duck or making a shallow dive to catch fish, squid, and invertebrates. One of the mainstays of the black-footed albatross diet around Hawaii is flying-fish eggs. Albatrosses, and their close relatives such as petrels and shearwaters, are well known for their sense of smell—they can smell fish oils from a great distance and will often come from over the horizon to feed on offal discarded from large fish boats. Who knows; it might have been our seasickness that piqued the curiosity of that albatross off Cape Scott. Conversely, most other birds can barely smell at all.

It was long assumed that all the albatrosses we see on the Pacific coast of North America between November and July are nonbreeding birds, but recent studies have shown that this is not completely true. Biologists have placed satellite radio transmitters on a number of black-footed albatrosses nesting on Tern Island in the French Frigate Shoals of western Hawaii. While the birds were feeding large young in spring and early summer, their two-week sojourns took them more than 4,000 kilometers eastward to the coast of North America. They spent a few days reaching the continental shelf, then a week or more feeding, primarily on squid. They then turned around and flew back to Tern Island, where they fed their chick for about twenty minutes, then flew out to sea, and repeated the journey.

Why do they make this tremendous flight? Well, firstly because they can. It takes relatively little effort for them to fly that distance, and their nestling can survive for several weeks on the last meal they delivered. Secondly, they do it because they have to. Only the rich upwelling currents along the Pacific coast provide the densities of squid they need to gather enough food for their nestling. If there were a suitable nesting island closer than Hawaii they would use it, but no candidates offer the combination of flat surface for the famously difficult albatross takeoffs and landings and lack of predators. So, although it was once thought that a few albatrosses used the Pacific coast as a post-breeding holiday location, it is actually a critical site for foraging while they are raising their young.

Because they wander the globe in their search for food, albatrosses are an ideal subject by which to monitor the marine ecosystems of the world. And all is not well—over the last thirty years the world's albatross populations have declined by about 40 percent. In 2003 the World Conservation Union listed the black-footed albatross as endangered based on projected losses in longline fisheries. The albatrosses follow fish boats and dive to take the bait fish off lines behind the boats—the birds become hooked and quickly drown. Some scenarios estimate that the black-footed albatross population may decline as much as 60 percent over the next three generations unless this problem is corrected.

Another problem is the predilection for albatrosses to pick up any bits of flotsam off the surface of the sea, including tremendous amounts of plastic. The adult birds can rid themselves of these bits of junk, but they feed a lot of it to their nestlings. A friend of mine once watched an albatross on Midway Island cough up a toothbrush for its young to eat. The young birds clearly suffer when a mass of plastic collects in their crop, and they don't have the strength to get rid of it.

There is a long-standing tradition among sailors that albatrosses are the embodiment of lost shipmates and friends. They certainly seem like sea spirits at times, silently and effortlessly banking over the waves and following ships on long ocean crossings. Let us hope they can guide us to a new appreciation of the unseen realm beneath the waters of the world.

BALD EAGLE

WHEN I WAS a fledgling biologist, fresh out of graduate school, one of the first contracts I took on was to conduct bird surveys on the Squamish River estuary. The Squamish flows out of one of the most rugged landscapes on the continent, draining a tumbled sea of rock and ice through deep green valleys. The valleys had been carved by huge glaciers during the Pleistocene and have narrow, flat bottoms and almost vertical sides of smooth rock. The river empties into Howe Sound, a fjord that had once been part of the Squamish Valley until the glaciers came, filling it with ice over a kilometer thick, pushing out to the Strait of Georgia. As the ice retreated about 12,000 years ago, the sea claimed the outer part of the valley, deepened as it was by the glacier. The Sound was born, and the new river mouth reformed farther up the valley, close to where the Cheakamus River flowed into the Squamish from the northeast.

Like all estuaries on the mountainous coast of British Columbia, the Squamish delta is extremely important for local wildlife and migratory birds and fish. It offers a rich oasis of mudflats, sedge marshes, and bottomland rain forest in an environment characterized by immense granite walls and deep, relatively sterile fjord waters. Estuaries on that coast also attract a special kind of animal—the human—drawn more by the prospect of flat building lots and protected anchorages than any richness of the land. My task was to repeat some surveys done a decade earlier in the early 1970s, to check what effects port expansion might have had on birds in the area, particularly on wintering waterfowl.

I had never really spent any time in the Squamish area before and was quickly taken by its beauty. Although I did most of my surveys in the winter, and the weather was often simply abominable, I was awed by the big green river flowing beneath the rocks and huge trees appearing out of the clouds, perched on the cliffs lining the valley. I was also impressed with the bird life and particularly liked to watch the trumpeter swans gliding quietly in the oxbows of the delta, their white bodies contrasting with the dark forest. But most of all I remember the eagles.

The Squamish River and its main tributary, the Cheaka-mus, like almost all rivers along the Pacific coast of north-western North America, are host to spawning salmon. Salmon runs up and down the coast attract all kinds of animals to the resultant feast of large dead and dying fish, from bears and gulls to ducks, loons, and dippers. But the stars of this wildlife spectacle, other than the salmon themselves, of course, are the bald eagles. All through the late summer and fall, eagles congregate along each spawning channel on the coast. As each run finishes, the eagles move on to a later run. And the latest run on the British Columbia coast is the chum

salmon run on the Squamish and Cheakamus rivers that happens in December and January.

Only a handful of rivers in North America have salmon in midwinter, and eagles flock from all over to gorge on the bodies. Bald eagles from Arizona and Wyoming that have fed on spawning kokanee in the Rockies join eagles from the Northwest Territories that have stopped off at the immense sockeye run in the Adams River, all drifting west to the Squamish, drawn by some ancient social memory, young birds following older veterans of the pilgrimage. By early January there are usually more than three thousand eagles along the river. Some big trees have fifty or more of the huge birds bending their branches. They remain there until the salmon bodies are gone, washed away by the winter monsoons, then move to the coast for the early spring herring spawn or another river for the eulachon runs. Bald eagles are nothing if not opportunistic and will travel many a mile for easy fishing.

Although they do catch a lot of live prey, bald eagles also have a scavenging heritage, being related to the vultures of Africa and Eurasia. They are not closely related to the golden eagle but are one of ten species of sea-eagles—big raptors that patrol the lakes and seashores of the world looking for waterfowl, fish, or anything that has washed up dead on the beach overnight. Benjamin Franklin famously argued that the turkey would be a better symbol of the United States than the bald eagle, citing the carrion-eating and even thieving habits of the bald eagle as unbecoming symbols of the new nation.

Over the years since the failure of Ben Franklin's (admittedly rather jestful) pro-turkey campaign, the bald eagle has become a symbol of power in the world, and its various short-comings are often glossed over. One shortcoming for such a power symbol is the eagle's wimpy call, which sounds a bit like a squeaky barbwire fence. The music video of "American Dream" by Crosby, Stills, Nash and Young opens with a magnificent soaring bald eagle, but when the eagle opens its mouth, out comes the scream of a red-tailed hawk.

More recently, the bald eagle also became a symbol of endangerment. For years, like all raptorial birds, the bald eagle was widely persecuted throughout its range. Then, after DDT was introduced into the world's ecosystems after World War II, it began to suffer a more insidious decline as the pesticide residues disrupted their reproductive systems, often producing eggshells so thin that they broke under the weight of the incubating birds. By the late 1960s there were fewer than five hundred pairs of bald eagles in the lower forty-eight states, a decrease of perhaps 99 percent from historic levels.

But the bald eagle came back. With the banning of DDT in North America in 1972 and serious population restoration programs, populations in eastern North America have increased by more than ten times, and those in British Columbia and Alaska, always the stronghold of the species, have gone up as well. Ironically, this success story has created problems for other birds. Double-crested cormorants, once an uncommon breeding bird in the Strait of Georgia, increased dramatically in numbers in the mid-1900s. The cause of this increase wasn't known, but when the benefits of the DDT ban hit home in the 1980s and '90s and eagle numbers increased on the British Columbia coast, cormorant numbers quickly declined to their 1920s levels. Nest predation by bald eagles is also blamed for similar declines in pelagic cormorant and great blue heron numbers on the British Columbia coast.

Bald eagles put a lot of effort into nesting. The nest itself is huge—about the size and shape of an inverted Volkswagen beetle, built near the top of a large tree. In treeless sites, such as on Triangle Island, British Columbia, bald eagles will build their nest directly on the ground. But there are no predators on Triangle fiercer than a mouse or rabbit, whereas eagles elsewhere have to contend with bears and such. The breeding cycle takes over five months—thirty-five days for incubation, two months for nestlings, and another two months when the young remain dependent on the adults after leaving the nest.

Once the young become independent, they can wander widely, seeking areas with high concentrations of food. Adults at northern breeding areas drift south on regular but individual migration routes to their favorite wintering ground. These migration routes almost always involve extended stopovers with easy food, such as the salmon runs mentioned above. Even adults breeding at southern locations will move north in the autumn to take advantage of such events before returning to their nesting territories in early spring. Early spring migrants through the western mountains stop at cattle ranches in February to clean up afterbirths left in the fields during calving.

The bald eagle's dramatic population recovery has made it the poster bird for successful conservation action. Many people are unaware how common the eagles are now; I used to lead bus tours to the eagle concentrations on the Squamish and Cheakamus rivers, and many participants were astounded when I pointed out single eagles soaring overhead as we drove through downtown Vancouver. But although the recovery has been surprisingly quick, it is still incomplete in several ways. Eagle populations seem healthy across eastern North America, but they are still only 10 or 20 percent of what they once were. Eagle nests across North America, even in the stronghold of British Columbia, are still failing because of high DDE (one of the common products of DDT breakdown) concentrations in the adult eagles. Other eagles die regularly from inadvertently consuming pesticides, heavy metals, and other poisons.

But perhaps the biggest threat to this aquatic raptor is the failing health of our lakes, rivers, and oceans. Hydroelectric projects have destroyed or irrevocably altered the aquatic ecosystems in most of our large rivers. On the West Coast, salmon runs are in a state of almost constant decline, and herring and eulachon numbers are worrisome as well. And the news of fish populations on the Atlantic coast is rarely less than catastrophic.

On August 25, 2005, a train derailment dumped 40,000 liters of sodium hydroxide into the Cheakamus River, killing thousands of fish. The spill devastated steelhead and rainbow trout populations in the river, but luckily most of the chum salmon, the main item on the menu of wintering eagles, were not in the river when the spill occurred. Whether this one spill will have any effect on chum populations won't be known until the adults return in 2008, but it is certainly an example of how one unexpected event could tip the balance against the bald eagle once again.

AMERICAN DIPPER

*H*ARDY FALLS IS one of my favorite spots for a short walk. I pull off a busy highway on the shores of Okanagan Lake, and within a few steps I am in a shady canyon. The roar of semi-trailers and oven-like heat of the tarmac are transmuted into the cool gurgling of Peachland Creek and sound of the wind swaying the ponderosa pines on the dry hills far above my head. Cottonwood down drifts through dappled sunlight into the lush green undergrowth of thimbleberry and Solomon's seal.

The trail winds back and forth, crossing the stream several times on small foot bridges. Water birches lean over the path, adding even more coolness on a hot spring day. Overhead, Vaux's swifts twitter as they circle their nest sites in the hollow trunks of the cottonwoods. I know other creatures are asleep in the trees as well; I once saw a screech-owl poking its head from one of the cottonwoods, its presence advertised by the mobbing cries of Steller's jays. The canyon soon narrows, and the big trees give way to the skies above where violet-green swallows chatter and Lewis's woodpeckers soar, both catching insects attracted to the cool valley.

If I keep walking, not tempted to stop and enjoy all this life around me, I reach the end of the trail in about ten minutes. There is Hardy Falls, a small yet impressive cascade off a rock wall into a deep green pool. I sit down on one of the benches and wait, my attention not on the falls themselves but on a lump of yellow moss under an overhanging rock near their base. Within a few minutes I see a gray bird, the size and almost the shape of a tennis ball, bobbing on the rocks in front of the moss. This bird is a dipper, and the moss clump is its nest. A cluster of mouths appear at the entrance to the nest, and the dipper stuffs insects into one of the hungry nestlings and flies off down the creek.

After the young have left the nest I often find one or more of the fledglings with a parent along the creek. The young constantly call, waving their wings and begging with wide-open mouths. The adult finds a caddisfly larva or some other such delicacy and pops it in the mouth, then turns to the creek and gives a short burst of song. The fledgling stops begging while the adult sings (both male and female give this special song) but starts wailing again as soon as the song stops. This post-feeding song is apparently the way the adults teach the young birds what dipper song sounds like. Most young birds learn the song of their species by hearing their father or neighbors sing in more normal situations, but young dippers may not be able to hear their fathers over the roar of the stream unless they are very close.

The dipper nest at Hardy Falls is a classic example of the form. Most dipper nests are built under overhangs on rock bluffs next to fast-flowing streams, and waterfall sites are favorites. Some nests are even built in crevices behind the falls so that the birds have to fly through the falling water to reach the nest. But waterfalls, or even rock bluffs, are not essential. There is a nest on the sluice gate of a small dam on the Okanagan River, and I have seen nests on the understructure of forestry bridges. My father once found a dipper nest built on a boulder in the middle of the Similkameen River; it was certainly protected from predators but wasn't safe from another river hazard. Luckily the young had already left the nest when it was swept away by the spring freshet in early June. Good nest sites are highly prized: one dipper nest site in Scotland has been used continuously for more than 120 years.

When the young become independent in midsummer they usually disperse out of the nesting territory, most flying upstream and many crossing the pass to the adjoining drainage. As winter freezes the high-elevation streams dippers move downstream, congregating along stretches of river with high concentrations of food. Like bald eagles and many other creatures, dippers especially like salmon or trout spawning grounds. There they gorge themselves not only on the fish eggs but also on the exceptionally rich invertebrate fauna that forms in these sites. Not surprisingly, one of the largest winter dipper concentrations in North America is found along the Cheakamus and Squamish rivers, home to one of the largest bald eagle concentrations as well. And the location that holds the Christmas Bird Count record for the highest dipper tally in North America is Lillooet, British Columbia, where almost all of the 150-plus dippers are seen along artificial spawning channels for salmon.

Dippers are most impressive in winter. It's hard not to admire a tiny songbird bobbing up and down on a boulder in the middle of an icy stream, singing its heart out. Close relatives of the wrens, dippers have a wonderful song. Over a hundred years ago, naturalist John Muir wrote that the song of the dipper

> is that of the streams refined and spiritualized. The deep booming notes of the falls are in it, the trills of rapids, the gurgling of margin eddies, the low whispering of level reaches, and the sweet tinkle of separate drops oozing from the ends of mosses and falling into tranquil pools.

And it's not just the songs and seemingly indomitable spirit of dippers that are inspiring—it's that they survive at all. Dippers catch their daily fare by diving into the water and literally flying below the surface, searching under stones and twigs for larvae huddled out of the fast-flowing current. To survive in winter they need the highest-quality waterproof coat, and indeed they have about twice the feather density of a land-bound songbird. Their almost spherical shape helps as well, reducing the surface-to-volume ratio critical for retaining heat. And they must eat constantly. I once watched a dipper pop out of a river and onto the ice around a rock, hauling a big clump of waterweed. It spread the plant material on the ice and carefully picked through it, much like my ecology students do when they are sampling aquatic insects from a dipnet. But whereas the task is mild drudgery to the students, it is life and death for the dipper. And some young dippers that disperse upstream find themselves trying to survive in places where the current can only manage to keep one hole open in the ice at air temperatures pushing -50°C.

There is a lucky pair of dippers year round at Hardy Falls. It must be one of the most sought-after territories in the dipper world, with an ideal nest site next to a rich food supply. Although the reach below the falls is only about 500 meters long, it is home to a spawning run of kokanee, the landlocked form of the sockeye salmon. Every September hundreds of red fish crowd the small stream, and loons and mergansers gather at the mouth to get their share of the catch. But doubtless the birds that are happiest to see the salmon return are the dippers, who reap the richness of the ecosystem every month of the year. And I feel that I harvest a bit of that bounty each time I walk that short trail.

AMERICAN COOT

A COUPLE OF YEARS ago I attended a Remembrance Day service in the Naramata community park on the shores of Okanagan Lake. A chilly wind was coming off the lake, but the sun occasionally beamed down between scudding clouds to light the waves on the bay and the last of the golden leaves flying off the big cottonwood trees. I positioned myself in the crowd so that I could watch the swaying trees and sparkling lake during the service even though it meant facing into the wind. I could see perhaps a hundred coots bobbing in the waves and made a mental note to get a good count of them after the service.

As a World War II veteran recounted his experiences in the invasion of Italy to the gathering, I couldn't help noticing another battle forming just offshore. The scattered flock of coots suddenly compacted itself with a dull roar, each bird skittering across the water surface toward the center of the flock. That coalescence could mean only one thing—an eagle was on the warpath—and in a few seconds it appeared. A young bald eagle swooped down on a single coot that had somehow missed the initial call to squeeze in with the rest of the flock.

The coot dove underwater to escape the eagle's attack, coming up a few feet closer to the flock, now packed so tight that there was no water visible at all between the sooty gray bodies. As the eagle turned for a second pass, the coot frantically paddled toward the flock but had to dive again as the talons descended. I thought for sure the coot was a goner—eagles are very good at harrying single ducks and coots until they are too tired to dive—but somehow it reached the safety of the flock before the eagle could snatch it from the surface.

Coots have always been familiar birds to me. When I was very young and just learning the art of birding by going out on Christmas Bird Counts, they were almost always the most abundant bird on the tally sheet at the end of the day. They appeared on the big local lakes in the fall, abandoning their nesting marshes on the prairies and plateaus before freeze-up. I usually saw them as distant flocks of bobbing blackish dots and was often given the task of counting them while my father searched the flock for more interesting ducks with our family's only pair of binoculars.

Very occasionally a cold snap would freeze the bays of Okanagan Lake; I remember walking out onto the ice one January to rescue a coot that had become stuck in the ice as it slept overnight. We kept it for a day or two in our bathtub, trying to make sure it was well fed before releasing it to rejoin its companions farther up the lake. That experience taught me that coots are very cantankerous and will bite sharply at the slightest provocation. That characteristic definitely shortened the time period we kept that bird in the bathroom.

Close up, coots are very strange-looking birds. They have battleship-gray bodies and blackish heads with striking white, chicken-like bills, ruby red eyes, and dark red foreheads. They swim with a pigeon-like bobbing of the head, and their short tails can stick up in a rather amusing way, but their strangest feature is their feet. Unlike most other water birds, which have webs between their toes, coots have lobes of scaly skin coming off each toe, so their foot surface is greatly expanded but the toes are not connected. Although they act superficially like ducks, swimming expertly on the surface of the water and diving to significant depths to get food, coots are not related to them or to the other common swimming birds. They are instead cousins to the rails and cranes, members of a marsh-dwelling family that have taken to open water for foraging.

In 1978 I spent six months on the Chilcotin Plateau of central British Columbia with my two brothers. Our job was to sample the aquatic insects in a series of small lakes and ponds on Becher's Prairie, a little bit of the Great Plains slipped in behind the Coast Mountains. Since the job was designed for one person, we got through our tasks quickly and had lots of spare time for exploring. We spent much of that summer wading through bulrushes looking for birds' nests. Red-winged and yellow-headed blackbirds were common—their nests made up a lot of our finds—and one lake had a colony of more than two hundred pairs of eared grebes that was a challenge to keep track of. But the easiest nests to find were coot nests—large platforms of reeds, usually with a ramp of marsh vegetation leading out of the water. We found them on big lakes and tiny ponds; all they seemed to need was a good stand of bulrushes or cattails and some deep water teeming with marsh life.

Coot nests were everywhere, and we soon found out why—each pair builds several platforms before choosing one to lay eggs in. The birds often begin incubating the eggs long before the clutch is complete, so the young hatch over a period of several days or a week. We noticed that many of the nests had two distinctly colored sets of eggs: one set might look dark, with large blackish splotches against the light tan background, whereas the other would have fine spots and appear quite light-colored. We speculated at the time that the different colors might relate to the timing of the egg laying, but I've since learned that it was probably because more than one female was laying eggs in that nest. These extra eggs are not particularly wanted by the incubating pair; the practice is called nest parasitism for good reason.

I saw a lot of young coots that summer, and if adult coots look strange the youngsters look positively psychedelic. They are little black downy balls with fluorescent scarlet beaks surrounded by orange down. This bizarre effect is capped off by a bald head covered with red skin except for patches of blue skin above the eyes. This kaleidoscopic combination is apparently necessary to stimulate parental behavior in the adults, which find the loudly peeping, flame-colored heads irresistible and constantly stuff aquatic insects into the orange mouths.

All those bugs make the young grow quickly, and they rapidly transform into gawky teenage coots, pale gray scruffy birds totally lacking both the fantastic plumage of the hatchlings and the eccentric elegance of the adults. The family groups gather into larger flocks and move off the small ponds to bigger lakes. One reason that coots are so successful and abundant is that they are able to dive underwater to reach food. They can therefore use a wide variety of aquatic habitats to find the marsh plants they normally feed on as adults and are especially common on big lakes after the nesting season is over.

By late summer the first groups begin leaving the breeding areas for wintering grounds, and more leave with every cold front that sweeps across the prairie marshes. Some move to coastal bays and estuaries, but most winter on big lakes that remain ice free. Like all members of the rail family, coots are strong fliers but take some effort to get airborne. They have to run across the water for some distance to gain take-off speed, a behavior known by the technical term—I am not making this up—of splattering, though some iconoclastic bird biologists apparently prefer the term spattering.

I know summer is over when I see a flock of coots scattered across the bay in front of the beach at Naramata. By early November there is a flock on almost every bay on Okanagan Lake. They often raft with diving ducks such as redheads, scaups, and canvasbacks, all species that feed on submerged water plants. The coots are expert divers but are not averse to stealing bits of food brought up from the depths by the ducks. The coots, in turn, are often taken advantage of by dabbling ducks such as wigeon. These birds can't dive but hang around flocks of coots and diving ducks to gobble up bits of milfoil and pondweed that the divers bring to the surface. And other birds are attracted to the flocks—whenever I stop to count a big flock I can usually spot a bald eagle perched on a big tree on the cliff above, surveying its winter larder.

BLACKPOLL WARBLER

I REMEMBER WELL MY first summer in the Canadian Rockies. I was working in Mount Robson Provincial Park and never grew tired of the awesome views—Mount Robson itself, a 3-kilometer-high wall of rock above the bluebird-blue waters of the Robson River. On one of my first days in the park I wandered along the river, where white spruce grew stunted in the silty soil. Over the rushing water I heard an unfamiliar bird song, a series of insistent, impossibly high notes. I searched out the source and saw a tiny warbler that looked a bit like a chickadee—mostly gray with a distinct black cap. I knew right away this was my first blackpoll warbler, an eastern species that doesn't venture into southern British Columbia where I grew up.

The one anecdote I remembered about the species, and one of the features that clinched the identification, was the high pitch of the song. Several books stated that it had the highest pitch of any North American songbird—older birders often lamented that it was the first bird to disappear from their soundscape, soon followed by other high-frequency songsters such as golden-crowned kinglets. When I got back to my cabin

I looked up blackpoll warblers in my field guide. I was struck by the interesting breeding distribution of the species—all across the boreal forest from Newfoundland to western Alaska—that didn't seem to line up with its migration route through easternmost North America.

That pattern is repeated time and again in migratory songbirds across North America. Birds I thought of as "eastern," such as the magnolia warbler, rusty blackbird, and least flycatcher, were actually northern species that didn't migrate south through the western valleys. Instead, they migrated north in spring to the boreal forests, then west to northern British Columbia, reversing their routes in fall. As a result, they were common birds of British Columbia that I never encountered while learning my birds in the Okanagan Valley.

That unfamiliarity reared its head a few years later when I was teaching a field ecology course in the southwestern Yukon, several hundred kilometers north of Mount Robson and farther west than almost anywhere in British Columbia. We were on the shores of Kluane Lake in another awe-inspiring landscape. To the east were the rolling alpine hills of the Ruby Range, to the west the highest peaks in Canada in the St. Elias Mountains. Massive glaciers such as the Kaskawulsh and Donjek flowed out of the largest non-polar ice cap in the world, their silty meltwaters feeding into the valley. And what a valley it was. Kluane Lake lies in the Shakwak Trench, part of the Denali Fault that arcs through Alaska from Bristol Bay to the Queen Charlotte Islands, reaching its apex and Mount Denali, the highest peak in North America.

At Kluane Lake the Shakwak Trench is a valley so immense that it has the tendency to dwarf the large mountains that line its western flank. It is a natural migration route for birds, and I kept looking up whenever I could to see what was passing by. Every morning several loons flew overhead on their way south, and the pebbly beach held new visitors—sandpipers and plovers—trading their Arctic breeding grounds for wintering areas in the tropics. One morning I was leading half the class in a bird census transect while my colleague Tony Sinclair was demonstrating mist-netting techniques for migration monitoring to the other students. As our group passed the nets, Tony called me over to look at an unfamiliar warbler. My pulse quickened as I looked at the relevant field marks—distinctly yellow head and breast, clear wing bars, and white tail spots. I had just come from a holiday in Connecticut, and this bird looked like an eastern species common there—the pine warbler. I couldn't believe that one would venture west to the Yukon, but couldn't think what else it could be. We took a lot of pictures documenting the plumage of the bird, then continued our censuses.

Back at the camp, I once again looked in *Birds of Canada* to see if there was anything else this bird could be. And there it was, staring off the warbler page—an immature blackpoll; completely different from the adults that I had seen years ago at Mount Robson. "Distinctive yellow feet," the book added, something that I remembered from the bird in Tony's hand. I felt somewhat embarrassed to admit to the students that our special bird was actually a species typical of the boreal spruce forests we were in. They learned something about the fallibility of professors that day, I imagine.

But that sighting further emphasized in my mind the curious migration route of the species. We were at 138°w at

Kluane, more than 400 kilometers west of the Queen Charlotte Islands, and here was a bird that would never think to
migrate to its winter home in South America by heading south
along the British Columbia coast. Instead, as I was later to
read, the blackpoll warbler has one of the most remarkable fall
migration strategies in the bird world.

Blackpoll warblers migrate north in spring from South
America by hopscotching across the Caribbean, then moving
north through the eastern United States. When they reach
the boreal forests of Canada, some turn east to Newfoundland
while others turn west to the northern Prairie Provinces, the
Yukon, and on to Alaska. In fall, these western populations
return via the same route, but then continue on to the Atlantic coast of Nova Scotia and New England. There they wait for
the right weather system—one that packs hefty winds out of
the northwest. When that arrives, they launch themselves up
and let the winds carry them out over the Atlantic.

They fly with the northwest winds until they meet the
northeasterly trade winds that carry them back toward land
in northern South America. This 3,500-kilometer route takes
the tiny birds about eighty-eight hours of nonstop flying to
complete. It is a risky business, of course—any change in the
weather could result in drowning in the sea—but those risks
must be outweighed by the risks of an overland route. In the
latter, winds are less help and the woodlands are full of hawks
and falcons looking for migrating birds to fuel their own migrations. The long flight requires fuel, of course; blackpolls leaving New England weigh about 21 grams, almost twice their
normal lean weight of 11 grams. They therefore can burn about

10 grams of fat to make the transcontinental flight, surely one of the most fuel-efficient journeys in the world.

Although the fall flight of blackpoll warblers is dramatic, it doesn't shed light on the question of why so may "eastern" species breed so far west yet do not migrate through the lush valleys of British Columbia and California on their way to Mexico. The answer to that question lies in genetics and the evolution of migration itself. Most—perhaps all—migratory birds have an innate direction and duration of migratory restlessness. They are literally programmed to fly southeast, south, or southwest for one week, two weeks, or two months, depending on the species. That direction and timing translates into a distinct migration route for each bird, a route that evolved over millennia as bird populations spread north as the Pleistocene ice sheets retreated.

As blackpoll warblers and other eastern forest species moved northward with the retreating ice, their western progress was blocked by the Great Plains until they reached the newly minted boreal forests of Canada. Successive generations followed those rich breeding grounds westward to northern British Columbia. Populations in the western cordillera, however, were blocked in their attempts to move northward by the massive ice sheets that covered southern British Columbia. These glaciers, fed by the same moist Pacific storms the West Coast is famous for today, took much longer to melt away than their counterparts on the prairies and in northern British Columbia. The boreal forests of the West, therefore, were first colonized by eastern species, and those birds were hard-wired to migrate east in fall to avoid the ice sheets of southern British Columbia and the treeless plains of central North America.

There is an old saying in comparative anatomy and embryology—"Ontogeny recapitulates phylogeny"—meaning that each developing embryo retraces the evolutionary steps that its species has taken. A human embryo, for instance, starts as a simple ball of cells, becomes a more complex form with a head and gut, growing gill slits, then loses the gills and takes on all the attributes of its adult parents. Annual migration routes of songbirds can also be thought of in this way—each bird retraces the steps taken by its species as it expanded its range following the retreating ice sheets. Blackpoll warblers, magnolia warblers, and rusty blackbirds are programmed to migrate east in fall before heading south, so they remain unfamiliar to birders like myself on the Pacific flyway. The few birds that stray from this path create excitement in the birding world but probably don't make much of an impact on the genetic makeup of the species as a whole.

WESTERN GREBE

*T*HE NORTH ARM of Okanagan Lake is about 15 kilometers long and represents only about a tenth of the lake's area. I like it because it is so different from the rest of the valley; the waters are shallow and warmer than the rest of the lake in summer, the eastern hills rolling and grassy rather than steep and rocky. But most of all I like it because it is wild. Homes and campgrounds are dotted along its western shores, but the eastern shores are, for the time being, relatively undeveloped. If you sit on the west side on a summer evening and look at the far hills, green-gold in the low sun, and if you squint a little, you can easily picture the valley as it was two hundred years ago, before the cows, before the orchards, before the malls.

I first explored the north arm in 1978, paddling a canoe along the shore, marveling at the big stands of cattails and bulrushes in the shallows. I flushed three bitterns that day and saw a black tern in graceful flight over the water—birds I rarely see elsewhere in the valley. My brother pointed out the tail of a coyote bouncing through the high grass, and we watched it stalk, unsuccessfully, a small flock of Canada geese, flightless in their summer molt. Clay-colored sparrows buzzed from rosebushes in the dry bunchgrass, the sound of the prairies in the middle of the mountains. Indeed, the marshes and grasslands gave the whole scene a certain prairie character, and we were there to look for a prairie bird: the western grebe.

Western grebes are the largest of their family in North America—elegant, long-necked water birds with a bright yellow, dagger-like bill. Like all grebes, they are excellent divers, feeding on small fish and large aquatic invertebrates. They are highly gregarious in both winter and summer. Western grebes nest in colonies on large, marshy lakes in western North America, many of them on the Canadian prairies. There are only three colonies in British Columbia; my brothers and I were checking on a relatively new colony that day in 1978.

We could pick out the grebes at a great distance, their swan-like necks dancing in the shimmer of the hot summer sun. We could hear them as well—the loud *cree-creet!* calls punctuating the quiet morning. Paddling along the east side of the arm we found three groups of nesting birds totaling about thirty-five pairs. The nests were typical for grebes: floating structures made from marsh plants piled on the water surface, usually anchored to adjacent bulrushes. The incubating birds slipped off the nests when we were still far away, piling nest material over the bluish-white eggs to keep them warm and hide them from marauding crows and gulls. As we carefully paddled by the nests the adults remained a discreet distance away, occasionally calling nervously.

It was a thrill to see these beautiful birds on their breeding grounds. Most of my previous experience with western grebes had been of wintering flocks on the protected inlets of the British Columbia coast. Shortly after I came back from a summer job to go to university in Vancouver, the grebes arrived as well. By November there would be thousands spread across English Bay, bobbing in the shallow swells around the dozens of freighters waiting to enter the harbor. While growing up I'd only seen migratory flocks passing through the Okanagan Valley. The spring migration can be spectacular; one day the lake is empty, the next morning there might be a thousand black-and-white shapes shimmering offshore, and two days later the lake is empty again.

I got to know western grebes much better in 1999 when the Ministry of Environment asked me to study their behavior and nesting success at three sites. The grebes had previously nested on Swan Lake near Vernon, but for some reason that colony had disappeared by the late 1970s. The colony on the north arm of Okanagan Lake seemed healthy enough, but the biggest colony was on Shuswap Lake at Salmon Arm just a half-hour's drive north of the other two sites. My task was to assess the three sites and suggest reasons why the colony at Swan Lake had failed.

I hired a student to do most of the field work but visited as often as I could to help in the censuses. We kayaked around the three sites, assessing habitat, sampling small fish stocks, counting boat traffic, and watching the birds. The Salmon Arm colony was built on both sides of a big marina, but the boats were directed out into the lake by a marked channel, and all boats, whether powered or not, were banned from the grebe colony areas. The nests were scattered along the lake-front in stands of reed canarygrass that were flooded as the lake level rose in early summer. As we paddled by the nests, we often saw the amazing courtship display in which the male and female approach each other in a very ritualistic way, then both suddenly race across the water side by side, their long necks held out before diving at the end of the long run. The grebes and their antics are such a popular attraction at Salmon Arm that the community holds an annual Grebe Festival. Another attraction for us at Salmon Arm was the large ring-billed gull colony at the eastern end of the bay; as we neared it the air would fill with white gulls, their calls mixing to form a loud chord of discontent.

I especially enjoyed kayaking around Swan Lake. Although it has houses along one side, almost all of Swan Lake is ringed by a rich marsh filled with birdlife. We saw hundreds of ducks, coots, and grebes on our surveys, and the air was always filled with clouds of swallows gorging themselves on midges emerging from the shallow waters. Red-winged and yellow-headed blackbirds called from the cattails. Swan Lake had everything except western grebes; although a few showed up early in the season, they disappeared before breeding.

What made them leave Swan Lake? All three sites had plenty of fish and nesting habitat; the only variable that seemed to differentiate them was the amount of boat traffic near the actual nesting areas. My conclusion was that western grebes were more sensitive to the presence of boats than other waterbirds. Red-necked grebes nest very successfully at all three sites, but they remained on their nests as boats went by, whereas the westerns slipped into the water whenever we approached. I think this habit increases the chance of nest predation by crows and gulls. The fact that the Salmon Arm colony can survive next door to a large gull colony suggests that they are disturbed very infrequently and remain on their eggs.

Colony nesting birds have very strong social instincts and are highly attracted to sites that already have plenty of birds. Perhaps a series of disturbances discouraged breeding at Swan Lake some time ago, and the birds found that Salmon Arm or Okanagan Lake were more reliable places to raise their young. We may never know.

What we do know is that the population of western grebes wintering on the Pacific coast of British Columbia and Washington has declined drastically in the last few decades. The big flocks on English Bay have disappeared; Christmas Bird Count totals have plummeted in Vancouver from fifteen thousand in 1970 to just twenty-eight in 2004. Overall, Christmas Bird Count totals for western grebes in British Columbia have declined by about 90 percent in the last thirty years. Counts in California have remained fairly stable, so there is a possibility that the birds have simply moved to more southern climes. Populations on the breeding grounds are poorly monitored in Canada, so we don't know if they are declining or not.

The likely cause of this change in wintering numbers lies beneath the surface of the water. Western grebes feed on small fish in winter, primarily juvenile herring. Herring numbers in turn are affected by sea temperatures, rising when the water is cold and nutrient-rich, falling when the water is warm and nutrient-poor. Since the 1970s sea-surface temperatures have been consistently warmer than average, and herring numbers have been low. This trend was briefly reversed in 2003 when sea temperatures were again cool, an event paralleled by a one-time increase in western grebe numbers. Biologists and birders will be keeping a close watch on western grebe numbers in the years to come; these beautiful birds are an important bellwether for the health of our oceans and lakes.

GRAY FLYCATCHER

*B*IRDING CAN BE a very competitive pastime. Most birders keep life lists—a tally of every species they've ever seen—and some get quite serious about checking their standing among their colleagues on that score. Others keep track of how many birds they've seen each year, an activity that can get quite expensive in both time and money if you're gunning for the North American Big Year title—a flight to Nome, Alaska, this weekend, the Dry Tortugas the next. I prefer the Big Day, a race of sorts to see which team can see or hear the most species in a single day. Big Days take a lot of planning to make sure one has designed the most efficient route, something that is a true test of one's local bird knowledge. They also favor those with keen ears and eyes that can pick out a rarity from the flock. But what I like best about them is that, unlike the Big Year or life list, they're over in twenty-four hours.

I started doing Big Days in 1979, driving from my parents' home in the Okanagan Valley to the Pacific coast at Vancouver. We would pick a good day in May when most of the breeding birds had returned from the tropics and a few Arctic nesters were still passing through. These events were a lot of fun, but they lacked real competition—we only had one carload of birders trying to see if we could beat last year's result. In 1986 I decided to challenge others to the game and founded the Okanagan Big Day Challenge. The rules were simple—get a team together and see how many birds each group can find in the Okanagan Valley on the Sunday of the Victoria Day weekend, then meet on Monday morning to pass out various trophies and exchange wild stories.

So, on May 18, 1986, I found myself racing down a gravel road east of Oliver in the Okanagan Valley of British Columbia with four friends. We had picked this road because it began near treeline, then descended through all the forest types before reaching the desert grasslands in the valley bottom. We could thus get most of the songbirds in the first four hours of daylight while they were singing, then spend the rest of the daylight hours looking for ducks, hawks, and a few other specialties.

It was about 7:30 AM as we neared the lower end of the ponderosa pine woodlands. We checked over our list to make sure we hadn't missed anything easy before leaving the forests—we didn't want to be saddled with the Sour Grapes Award. "Dusky flycatcher," someone said. "We still haven't seen a dusky flycatcher." That was surprising—the dusky flycatcher was one of the commonest birds in the valley. We had to stop before we ran out of pines. I pulled the car over at a cattleguard, and we all leapt out. Immediately I said "There's one!" as I heard the distinct calls of a flycatcher. We were all ready to jump back in the car, but something made us stay a few seconds longer—the call hadn't been quite right.

I listened more carefully as the bird continued to sing *chelep chelep, chelep sweet!* I suddenly realized this bird was not a dusky flycatcher but its close relative, the gray flycatcher. Both birds could easily win the Drabbest Bird on the Continent Award but they have slightly different habitat requirements and distinct calls—the dusky flycatcher says *sidit kwerp sweet!* What was amazing about seeing a gray flycatcher in the Okanagan Valley was that the species had never been found breeding in Canada before. In fact, there was only one accepted record for the country—an off-course migrant banded in Toronto in 1981. They were birds of the juniper-sagebrush deserts of the Great Basin; I had only seen them on their wintering grounds in northwestern Mexico.

I grabbed the tape recorder, and we all converged on the bird for a better look. I managed to get a reasonable recording of the song, and after thirty minutes of documenting the sighting we climbed back in the car, elated at our discovery but also worried we had wasted a lot of time that might cost us dearly in species at day's end. The next morning we gathered with the five other teams that had been out. I proudly announced that we would undoubtedly win Bird of the Day honors, to which my brother Syd replied "Did it say *chelep chelep*?" Amazingly, his team had seen a gray flycatcher at another site. In fact, two members of his team recounted how they were sure they had seen one two years ago at exactly the same spot we had seen ours; unfortunately it had not called, so they couldn't convince others of the sighting.

The day after the discovery, our friend Norm Chester-field flew out from Ontario to see the bird—he had the big-gest list of Canadian birds as well as the biggest life list in the world at that time. On June 1 we made a careful search of the area and were surprised to find thirteen gray flycatchers singing. This was indeed a serious invasion.

I immediately began some library research to find out what was going on with gray flycatchers, and a fascinating story soon emerged: in the late 1960s some left their tradi-tional shrub steppe habitat to colonize the ponderosa pines of northeastern California and central Oregon. They seemed to like these woodlands, which lacked any other flycatcher; dusky flycatchers were found in shrubby areas in ponderosa pine for-ests but tended to avoid pure patches of the trees. Gray fly-catchers quickly spread north, following the narrow band of ponderosa pine forests on the east side of the Cascades, reach-ing Washington by 1972. By 1980 they were in the Methow Valley, only 75 kilometers south of the Canadian border. So our birds were part of this long march north.

After several surveys of the Okanagan Valley to see where gray flycatchers had settled, a clear picture of their preferred habitat emerged. The birds were breeding in stands of rather young ponderosa pines with little or no understory. This envi-ronment had changed radically through the 1900s as selective logging took out all the big pines and fire suppression pro-moted the growth of small pines. Once gray flycatchers dis-covered this new habitat they flourished and their progeny followed the pines north. The young pines were only slightly bigger than the junipers of the Great Basin, and the woodlands were still open enough to allow the flycatchers' main feeding technique—flying to the ground from low branches to pick off bugs in the grass.

In the twenty years since our initial discovery the species has not spread much farther; the northernmost records are now from Kelowna, only an hour and a half's drive north of Oliver. The population seems contained by the boundaries of suitable habitat—extensive young ponderosa pine forests. They haven't made the jump into the ponderosa pines of Thompson Valley to the north, perhaps blocked by thick Douglas-fir forests in the low passes.

Gray flycatchers have taught me a few things about birds and the world in general. Firstly, although they have wings and can fly, birds rarely move beyond places where they have been found in the past. They are creatures of habit, often tied by genetically controlled behaviors that keep them coming back to the place of their birth. The rapid range expansion of gray flycatchers is an extremely rare event in the bird world but is an example of what can happen if a species discovers a habitat change and makes the leap to take advantage of it. Secondly, there is nothing static about nature: things are always changing, and too often these days we humans are the authors of that change. We can never predict what the consequences of altering the environment might be, and the next event may well be more serious than a sudden influx of small, drab birds.

The Okanagan Big Day Challenge remains a popular event with birders every spring. It is now run as a fundraiser for bird conservation and research and so has a practical side as well as being pure fun. And yes, we did eventually hear a dusky flycatcher on that inaugural Challenge and managed to win the Flammulated Owl Award for most species on the day—156.

TURKEY VULTURE

*T*HE THRONE IS an imposing bluff at the north end of Osoyoos Lake in the Okanagan Valley. Its component rock is some of the oldest in British Columbia: sediments laid down along the western shore of an ancient North America, then buried by an island mass that collided with the continent about 180 million years ago. The sedimentary rocks were metamorphosed into hard gneiss kilometers below the surface of the earth, then exposed once again as the Okanagan Valley cracked open about 55 million years ago. The Throne looks more Arizonan than Canadian, cloaked in a sparse growth of grass, sagebrush, and scattered ponderosa pines, overlooking sandy benchlands covered in antelope-brush and brittle prickly pear cactus. It is a favorite spot for visiting birders, who enjoy the dramatic views as much as the resident canyon wrens, chukar, and golden eagles.

The southern side of The Throne rises in a steep rock wall about 300 meters high, but on the west side there is a small plateau about a third of the way up—the seat of the throne. One warm summer day in the 1970s my father decided to climb up to this plateau to look at the condition of the grasslands there. He felt that the surrounding rock walls would have discouraged cattle from grazing this small area and it might be the only patch of native grasslands in the Okanagan that remained in pristine condition, providing a glimpse of what these special desert grasslands were like before ranching came to the Valley in the 1860s.

He quickly found himself on the plateau and was impressed by the health of the grass there. Continuing on, he struggled up the steep slopes to the summit. The view was spectacular, so he took a few photographs and decided to reward his efforts with a short nap in the hot sun. He quickly drifted off to sleep but was startled awake sometime later as a shadow passed over his face. Opening his eyes he saw a turkey vulture hanging in the air only a few feet above him. The bird was obviously taking a close look to assess whether my father was dead or alive and soared off with the wind when he stirred.

Turkey vultures certainly fit in with the semi-desert landscape of The Throne. Their bright red heads give them a decidedly tropical, or perhaps simply alien look; these featherless heads also give them their name. Vultures also have grotesquely large nostrils; in fact, if you look through the nostril on one side of the bill you can see daylight out the other side—it is simply one big hole through the base of the bill. Some biologists feel that this feature is a mechanical adaptation that reduces the chance that the nostrils will get clogged by bits of rotting meat as the bird dives into a carcass; if a tasty morsel gets stuck, a quick shake of the head will dislodge it if the hole is big enough. But it may also enhance the air flow into the nostrils, a distinct advantage for the vultures' sense of smell.

Most birds have a very poor sense of smell, but turkey vultures are clearly an exception to that rule. Field experiments have shown that turkey vultures can find relatively small dead animals that are completely hidden from view by smell alone. One of the chemicals they seek out is mercaptan, a foul-smelling group of compounds given off by decaying organic matter, including bodies. Mercaptan is often added to odorless natural gas for safety purposes, and gas companies have discovered leaks in pipelines by observing flocks of vultures soaring over certain sections of line.

Vultures are designed for soaring flight, with very large wings in proportion to their light body. They fly with their wings held in a distinctive V-shaped tilt, gently rocking back and forth in the air currents. Long primary feathers spread out like fingers at the wingtips, reducing turbulence and drag, allowing the vultures to soar effortlessly for hours. This talent is clearly valuable if you're looking for uncommon food items like dead bodies.

Turkey vultures have a fascinating habit that helps them survive the tropical heat: instead of perspiring as we do or panting like a dog, they defecate on their legs. This behavior, technically known as urohydrosis, is highly effective because the legs have a lot of blood vessels near the surface that are cooled as the moisture evaporates off the wet legs. So if you see a vulture soaring with its legs hanging down, you know it's just cooling its wet heels.

Although vultures can handle heat well, they don't particularly like the cold. Whether it's keeping those delicate legs warm or smelling and consuming frozen roadkill, vultures' thoughts turn southward in September, and they migrate en masse to Central and northern South America. Small groups, or kettles as they are called, can be seen tilting southward, occasionally gathering into larger groups where large bodies of water need to be crossed or avoided. One such place is near Sooke on the southern end of Vancouver Island, where flocks of up to a thousand vultures can be seen soaring in late September, waiting for favorable winds to cross Juan de Fuca Strait. More than ten thousand vultures move southwest along the north shore of Lake Erie in early October, rounding the lake at the mouth of the Detroit River. By November most of the migrant vultures converge on Panama, where hundreds of thousands pass overhead in a river of raptors on their way to the savannas of Venezuela and Colombia.

In my childhood turkey vultures were considered a rather special bird in southern British Columbia; I remember being astounded by a flock of twelve one evening at The Throne. When I moved back to the Okanagan thirty years later I was surprised to find an equal number roosting in the Douglas-firs behind my new home for much of the summer. I found another similar roost behind a soccer field my son played at and a third near the local airport. Vultures were obviously doing well in British Columbia. In fact, turkey vulture populations have been increasing throughout Canada and much of the United States since about 1980. There are probably several causes for this increase. Vultures, like other large birds at the top of the food chain, were significantly affected by reproductive failure caused by DDT in the mid-1900s, so the banning of DDT in 1972 undoubtedly has improved breeding success. But vultures are definitely moving north as well, perhaps motivated by increasing deer populations, deforestation, and global warming.

The Throne was declared an ecological reserve by the provincial government in 1980 after a fifteen-year campaign that my father and his colleagues waged. The reserve extends from the peak of the mountain to the benchlands below and south to the marshy shores of Osoyoos Lake. At that time, The Throne was surrounded by desert grasslands, and many land managers wondered why we needed to set aside this particular sample. Today it is an island in a sea of grapes planted to supply the burgeoning wine industry. Like vultures, grapes are moving north as well, as longer summers and later frosts allow the cultivation of noble varieties such as cabernet sauvignon and syrah in the south Okanagan. Vultures still soar over The Throne, but they probably have to pass over the vineyards to search for their carrion higher in the hills.

Date D